THE MAGIC WHIP

OTHER BOOKS BY WANG PING

American Visa, short stories, Coffee House Press, 1994

Foreign Devil, a novel, Coffee House Press, 1996

Of Flesh & Spirit, poems, Coffee House Press, 1998

New Generation: Poetry from China Today, Hanging Loose Press, 1999

Aching for Beauty: Footbinding in China,
University of Minnesota Press, 2000; Random House, 2002 (paperback)

The Magic Whip

POEMS BY WANG PING

COFFEE HOUSE PRESS

2003

Poems from *The Magic Whip* have appeared in the following journals, anthologies, and newspaper: *XCP: Cross Cultural Poetics; Indiana Review; Luna; Facture; The World; GSU Review; Speakeasy; Global City Review; Bombay Gin; The KGB Bar Book of Poems,* David Lehman and Star Black, editors; *Exhibition Under Construction,* May Joseph and Mark Nowak, editors; *Hanging Loose; Manoa, Minneapolis Star Tribune; Water-stone,* and *The Butcher Shop.*

My thanks to the following people and many others whose help and love are invaluable in every possible way: Robert Bly, Cathy Bowman, Jim Dawes, Kate DiCamillo, Steve Dickison, Clayton Eshleman, Patricia Weaver Francisco, Jim Dawes, Ray Gonzalez, Kimiko Hahn, Sandy Benitez Kondrick, Lorna Landvik, Judy LaVercombe, Alex Lemon, Adam Lerner, Walter Lew, Rich Linngren, Zachary Marell, Sue Marquis, Christopher Mattison, Alison McGhee, Mark Nowak, Ren Zhuoling, Ron Padgett, Mary Rockcastle, Jerod Santek, Julie Schumacher, Bart Schneider, Chris Spohn, Faith Sullivan, Tom Wallace, Lewis Warsh, Chris Welsch, Michelle Wright.
    Special thanks to Allan Kornblum and Chris Fischbach who edited the manuscript with great insight and enthusiasm, Josie Rawson and Molly Mikolowski who worked hard to make the book available to the public, Linda Koutsky for her graphic production work, and the rest of the Coffee House Press staff.

Coffee House Press books are available to the trade through our primary distributor, Consortium Book Sales & Distribution, 1045 Westgate Drive, Saint Paul, MN 55114. For personal orders, catalogs, or other information, write to: Coffee House Press, 27 North Fourth Street, Suite 400, Minneapolis, MN 55401.
    Coffee House Press is a nonprofit literary publishing house. Support from private foundations, corporate giving programs, government programs, and generous individuals help make the publication of our books possible. We gratefully acknowledge their support in detail in the back of this book.

Library of Congress CIP Information
Wang, Ping
The magic whip : poems / by Wang Ping. — 1st ed.
p. cm.
ISBN 1-56689-147-7 (ALK. PAPER)
1. Chinese American women—Poetry. 2. Women—China—Poetry.
3. Tibet (China)—Poetry. 4. China—Poetry. I. Title.

PS3573.A4769M34 2003
811'.54—DC21
2003055094

1 2 3 4 5 6 7 8 9
First Printing | First Edition

Printed in the United States

CONTENTS

FOR ADAM, ARIEL, AND LEO

THE MAGIC WHIP

for Chris

It is the mark of
a virgin,
the *yellow blossom girl*
men would bid
to deflower—the black pigtail
that brushes its path
along the waist, hips, backs
of the knees, tied with
a ribbon or red yarn.

"No woman is allowed to bind her feet and every Chinaman must wear a queue,"
ordered the first emperor of Qing.

I saw the black down on my shins,
thought I was turning into a man.

She trades her voice for human legs, rises naked from the sea to meet the prince
on the beach. She wraps her shame with a cloak of brown hair that drapes to the
ankles. I cried over the book stolen from a sealed library, and vowed to keep my
hair long.

I poured the kerosene into a wooden basin, and let go of my braids. "Are you
sure you want to do this?" asked the old village woman who gave me the folk
recipe. "Another way to get rid of those bugs, once and for all, is to shave your
hair." I nodded, bent my head, and slid the black cascade into the kerosene.
Fumes smarted my eyes and pricked the scalp like needles. Count to three hun-
dred and all the lice and the eggs will be dead, I muttered through clenched
teeth. I was fifteen, had just left home to work on the village farm. I was deter-
mined to save my hair, at any cost.

She combed her daughter's hair,
coiled it into a bun, crisscrossed
with strings of pearl, velvet flowers,
a golden hairpin of the phoenix
to hold it tight.

The husband came to fetch her.
Kneeling on the bed, she licked
a hole through the paper window,
watched him carry her youngest girl
into a bridal sedan, face wet behind
a scarf. She wanted to join
the wailing to wish her good luck.
But she had no more tears.

When they caught the adulterers, the villagers broke the man's legs and plucked
the woman's pubic hair clean.

After midnight
the only lights are from the beauty
salons along DeKalb Avenue
of Brooklyn where they braid
each other's kinky hair
laughing, slapping their thighs.

In Hong Kong, she cut the braids she'd kept for fifteen years. She arrived in JFK
the next day, the new C-bob perched on her scalp like a battered helmet.

The Chinese Boxers braided talismans into their queues.
We have magic whips, they sang in unison.
No bullets from the foreign ghosts
can ever touch us.

A woman without pubic hair is called a "white tiger"—a man killer.

Hair curling up over his shirt
buttons, hair running down the back
of his neck, hair rolling out of his sleeves,
hair on his legs when he comes
dripping from the ocean.
And he's my "honey," my "sweetheart,"
my "daddy."

She caught him again with a woman in their bedroom. "I can't go on like this. You keep the son and I'll take care of this one," she pointed to her swollen womb, and left. Within a week, her hair became matted and the braids formed into the shape of a cobra with a raised hood, lice in the locks like worms. No man would go near her.

Tough hair on a girl equals stubbornness equals disobedience equals bad luck.

His advice to women friends:
Keep your hair long
if you want to find a man.

"I'm so tired of my hair. I'm ready to cut it," I whined to my lover.
"If you cut it," he said sternly, "you'll have nothing left."

Another outbreak of lice in the nursery. Teachers pulled her out to examine her head. They always started with her, for some reason. They didn't know that lice hated kinky hair. Its nappy jungle made it too difficult to reach the scalp for blood.

The laws of the Great Qing: removing a man's queue is punishable by decapitation.

He caught me shaving with his razor at 3:00 A.M.
"I thought Chinese were hairless," was all he could say.

The nurse shaved her, told her to relax. The doctor walked in, face behind a mask. He injected anesthesia into the naked armpits, then cut along the marks drawn on the skin. He peeled. She felt the tugging and pulling, her arms jerked up and down like a puppet. He finished the last stitch. "All gone. No more sweat, no more fox stink," he said cheerfully. "Are you really eighteen?" he examined her face. She looked up at his sparse eyebrows, couldn't tell him she was fifteen but had already smelled so bad that nobody would come close, couldn't tell him she had to sell her pet chickens to pay for this. "I know it's none of my business," he said. "But if you are younger, the sweat glands may grow back and you'll need another operation."

I grew up hearing this every day:
A man without a mustache
is a man without a brain.

Names for haircuts: crimp, bangs, snake mane wave, curlicue, buzz cut, spike, coif, upsweep with attitude, brow-tossing, ringlet-topped, shoulder-brushing, tousle-finish, wind-blown, dred-like, razor-cut, luscious body, hip with a flip, down-to-there.

When the last Qing Emperor was dethroned, the New Republican soldiers patrolled the streets and shaved off men's queues.

A treatment for hysteria: depilation of pubic hair. When blood rushes to the pulled roots, the "heated" head will cool down.

She got a perm at Midtown Hair. Her lover opened the door and laughed. "Where did you get that Afro cut?" The next day, she found a Korean salon in Flushing, and straightened all the curls. She ate Ramen, ten cents a package, for the rest of the month.

Hairpainting	Colorsilk	Natural Instincts	Nice 'n' Easy
Les Rouge	Nutrisse	Color Shock	Gray Chic
Xtreme FX	Consort	Born Blond	Just for Men

Women constantly stop her on the street and say,
"I love your braid.
Don't ever cut it."

The body dies, but the hair continues to grow.

AFTER THRASHING ABOUT,
BUT NOT VIOLENTLY

I have tried to write paradise.
The words have faded, so have the author
and the artist who copied them with colored pencils.

Sounds of objects hurling through space—
flickering lights from the dark matter
of remembrance.

Who's to say that my thought,
occurring at this moment, can't be yours
from light-years ago?

You filmed me jumping puddles under the neon lights
of 42nd Street. "What is that?" frowned the Japanese dancer.
"What is she doing in your film?"

Time is a sequence of brutal insults to the mind. No?
The ladder is broken at its waist, the sound of bells
from the ocean floor, yellow crystals filtered through the air.

I dreamt I sat on a frozen lake, searching
through the mist for a tree. Behind me you loomed
on tiptoes, the moon casting our shadows toward the shore.

The notion that not everything has to make sense—
this could be a mask for my lack of taste, intelligence.
How should I find solace in such ambiguity, such stubbornness?

The wind still blows within the frame,
this way, that way, this way again.
Let those I love try to forgive what I have made.

Words reel in loops—an invisible shuttle combing my warped hair.
Let's make a scandal.
Let's embrace as if there were no tomorrow.

MIXED BLOOD

At fifteen, my father ran away from his widowed mother to fight the Japanese.

"I'll come back with a Ph.D. and serve my country with better English and knowledge," I pledged at the farewell party in Beijing.

Home— 家 —*jia:* a roof under which animals live.

> When asked where I'm from,
> I say "Weihai," even though
> nobody knows where it is,
> even though I've never been to that place.

He lost his left ear in a bayonet fight with a Japanese soldier. Two years later, American cannons split his eardrums.

The night I arrived at JFK, the Mets won the World Series and the noise on the street went on till three. I got up at six and went to work in my sponsor's antique shop in Manhattan.

The bag lady stopped her cart on the busy street and peed onto a subway grate.

"Did you jump or fly?" asked my landlady from her mah-jongg table. Then she laughed and told me that her husband had jumped ship ten years ago. When he opened his fifth Chinese take-out, he bought her a passport and flew her to Queens.

The only thing he liked to talk about was his old home, Weihai, its plump sea cucumbers and sweet apples, men with broad shoulders, stubborn thighs, and girls with long braids making steamed bread.

"I don't know why," she said, shivering behind her fruit stand. "Back home, I could go for days without a penny in my pocket, and I didn't feel poor. Now, if my money goes down below four figures, I panic." She scanned the snow-covered streets of Chinatown. "I guess I really don't want to be homeless here."

I hired the babysitter when she mentioned that her hometown was Weihai.

The president visited the rice paddies in Vietnam where a pilot had been downed thirty-three years ago.

My father tried to return to Weihai after his discharge from the Navy. With his rank, he could find work only in a coalmining town nearby. My mother refused to go. He went alone, and soon contracted TB. Mother ordered me to date the county administrator's son so my father could come home.

> "No, I'm not sad." The street kid shook her head.
> "How can I miss something I've never had?"

On her sixtieth birthday, my grandma went home to die. She would take two ships, one from the island to Shanghai, then from Shanghai to Yantai. From there, she would take two buses to reach Weihai. I carried her onto the big ship at the Shanghai Port, down to the bottom, where she'd spend three days on a mattress, on the floor, with hundreds of fellow passengers. "How are you going to make it, Grandma?" I asked. She pulled out a pair of embroidered shoes from her parcel and placed them between my feet. "My sweetheart and liver, come to see your old home soon, before it's too late."

House— 房 —*fang:* a door over a square, a place, a direction.

He never lost his accent, never learned Mandarin or the island dialect.

> Weihai, a small city
> in Shandong Province,
> on the coast of the North China Sea,
> a home, where my grandfather
> and his father were born,
> where my grandma married,
> raised her children, and
> now lies in the yam fields,
> nameless, next to her husband,
> an old frontier to fend off Japanese pirates,
> a place I come from, have never seen.

Back from America, my mother furnished her home on the island, bought an apartment in a suburb of Shanghai, and is considering a third one in Beijing. "A cunning rabbit needs three holes," she wrote to her daughters, demanding their contributions.

They swore, before boarding the ship, that they'd send money home to bring more relatives over; in return, they were promised that if they died, their bodies would be sent back home for burial.

> I drink American milk—a few drops in tea.
> I eat American rice—Japanese brand.
> Chinese comes to me only in dreams—in black-and-white pictures.

My mother buried her husband on the island, where he lived for forty years.

Room— 屋 —*wu:* a body unnamed and homeless until it finds a destination.

> We greet a stranger with,
> "Where are you from?"
> When we meet a friend on the street, we say,
> "Where have you been? Where are you going?"

家—a roof under which animals live
房—a door over a square, a place, a direction
屋—a body unnamed and homeless until it finds a destination

> —my tangled roots for home.

FIRST STEP

Like swans lifting from the river in frozen mist,
like the first ice splitting the shore of Lake Superior,
you took a step, then another.

A laughing Ariel!
Your smile is not a mask but a shrieking delight—
a horizon expanding
between your wobbling feet.

The meadow is full of traps—
long-stemmed flowers, spiky grass,
lumps of soil, rocks.
A gust of wind blew your cap,
sent it rolling toward the sea.

Hands open,
a crowd of angels cradled in your bosom,
you stumble
into the arms of air, wind, sun, earth . . .

without looking back.

ON THE OTHER HAND

The horse woman in a corset whispers orders
on stage, waving a black quirt. At solstice

night, rain and hail, peonies bend their heads into
the earth, and clematis climbs over the neighbor's

fence, regardless. Thunder, tipped-over sky,
dreams split, close. She wakes with a premonition

throbbing at her temples. Open your limbs,
he replies, soak up light before winter comes

full blast. Who told you influenza comes from Asia,
where animals and birds live under the same roof

with humans? Can't stand them, she moans,
those photogenic people, always complaining about

their faces! And the escaped Asian carp
in the Mississippi, would electric nets slow

down the invasion? So Mr. Seng is neither Chinese
nor Indian, but an angular Berliner with sauerkraut

on his breath? Rules don't always count, he says
patiently, lining fallen petals along the window-

sill. Beauty is top-heavy, so is ugliness.
Surrender yourself under the river of stars

on the shortest night. Watch them jump, those smooth-faced
carp from Asia, breaking fishermen's noses, wiping out

plants in the lake. No, I don't have a crush.
I only think about her when I cross a river, or sit with buffalo.

OUR TEACHER OF MARXISM

The boy did it again. When we opened our rice boxes, frogs, scorpions, and worms crawled out. We showed the ruined dinners to his adopted father, our teacher of Marxism and Leninism. He exempted our midterm test as consolation.

That night, the whole dormitory heard it—soles hitting a bare bottom. The homemade cotton shoes were easy to grab, the boy had told us. They hurt the skin and flesh, but not the bones. The teacher moaned with each thrashing—high-pitched like cats in heat. The boy remained quiet.

We lay in our bunk beds, hands on grumbling stomachs. The pumpkin-faced urchin caused endless grief for our favorite teacher, who had adopted him after the boy's father, a poverty-stricken peasant, died. We heard he'd wanted to marry his brother's widow to care for her children, but his wife, who also taught Marxism, refused a divorce. She lived with their ten-year-old daughter in another city. It was said our teacher visited them once a year, in the summer. He spent the rest of his days and nights checking our political and physical health, teaching us how capitalism exploited the poor, women, children, how we must fight for justice, organizing activities to raise our social consciousness. He stoked our enthusiasm by giving us extra credit to memorize *The Manifesto* and chapters from *Das Kapital*. Everyone received his highest grade—120.

We knew this was necessary to turn the boy around. We'd gone through the same ourselves, at home, in kindergarten. Still, it was hard to listen. Each thrash hit our nerves, brought out memories.

The next morning, the boy greeted us pleasantly in the canteen. He looked rested. A girl asked, "How did the soles taste?"

"Great. Like pancakes."

She grinned. "Aren't you homesick?"

To our surprise, he started weeping. "This is my home. My uncle never flogs me with buckles or bamboo twigs. And I can play all day, eat as much as I want, rice and meat. What more can I ask for?"

BOMBS, ORANGE, BAGS OF RICE

Make bombs   make bombs   toys of the universe   A-bombs   H-bombs
missiles   precision-guided   3,000   within 2 days   threat   shock them
awe them   bomb the shit out of   teach a lesson for not complying   specta-
cles on TV   satellites   radios   just watch   all the media   comply   threat
wash brains   compassion   truth   a lie repeated a hundred times   becomes
truth   "what we need is"   bombs   hospitals   schools   power stations
spectacular   bodies flung out of Baghdad   exploding over Istanbul   grander
than July 4th fire   what to tell children   threat   screaming mothers   babies
on cindered breasts   "what we need is"   mutilated animals   Baghdad in ash
how to tell children   compassion   threat   repeat a hundred times   there
won't be a voice after this   not a spirit left for fighting   hell   this bag of **rice**
how did it get here?   threat   x-ray it   irradiate   shock and awe   "what
we need is"   nations   people   standing against   rally   freedom of speech
beautiful   such democracy   rally   ye prisoners of want   bombs   Patriot
Act I   CIA back in business   FBI   homeland   espionage   domestic surveil-
lance   immigrants   aliens   threat   colored   bearded   anyone who can't
afford   strip   strip them   rights   citizenships   open mouths   deport
take down power   cut water   cut taxes   cut   physically   emotionally
psychologically   respectful of human rights?   read my   threat   compassion
"what we need is"   Congress   what Congress   this war   personal   family
business   finishing an old grudge   "what I need is"   blood thirst?   war-
monger?   oil?   nothing to do   literally nothing to do with compassion
after repeated a hundred times   truth   morally superior   our duty to liberate
to bomb   comply   or threat   another bag of **rice**   hey   make sure it
doesn't happen again   or you'll be   see my toys?   A-bombs   H-bombs
electrons   rip into earth   rip bellies   oh my naughty thunderbolts   how
can I hate what's needed to love?   to make history?   leap   my sports
bounce and frolic   bomb China   bomb Japan   bomb Korea   "what we
need is"   bomb Guatemala   Indonesia   Cuba   **rice** again?   bomb **rice**
bomb Vietnam   Laos   Congo   bomb Peru   threat   bomb Guatemala
Cambodia   O bomb   let me kiss your tail   eat your boom   boom ye El
Salvador   boom ye Nicaragua   Grenada   what great songs you make
boom   boom sun and moon   boom boom economy   every explosion a
boost to my   stimulus package   threat   what to tell children   backbones
"what we need is"   protect America   boom Libya   Panama   and bye-bye Iraq

Sudan   boom Afghanistan   boom Yugoslavia   **rice**   bags of **rice**   arrive
in hundreds   shameful politics   bomb   *in how many of these instances did a
democratic government, respectful of human rights, occur as a direct result? Choose one
of the following*   fuzzy math again?   listen up   here's the truth under oath
nothing but   0   zero   zilch   none   not a one   a whole number
between -1 and +1   repeat a hundred times   threat   hey   cover that damn
tapestry   that propaganda   Guernica 1937   Spain   axis of evil   Picasso
shrieking horses   bulls   mothers bent over broken babies   1,600   bomb
the shit out of   Nazi planes   shock and awe   teach them a lesson   physically
those damned Basques from Guernica   carpet-bomb them   emotionally   for
resisting Franco   General Franco   not France Franco   that Europe   that
old fart   break their spirit   psychologically   on behalf of Franco   what to
tell children?   "There will not be a safe place in Baghdad"   is what to tell
O Christ   **rice**   where's Tom?   hey   cover that fucking tapestry with blue
backbones   for cameras   comply   compassion   my Secretary of State's
head   must not speak   threat   next to a screaming horse   writhing
hands with flayed fingers   light bulb   bombia   bomba bambia   bomb
how to tell   threat   3,000 missiles   in first 48 hours   better than the nuke
over Hiroshima   faster   nothing left after   zero   "what we need is"
Powell's head   clean   before the Security Council   against the blue curtain
his evidence of   threat   noncompliance   WMD   anthrax   depleted ura-
nium in breathable bits   **rice**   Christ   not again Tom   Tom boy   vaca-
tion over   do something   it's getting annoying   duct tape   not funny
gas   sarin   mustard   mustard   **rice**   Tom what did you do with the bil-
lions I gave   ohohoh   surveillance on phones   internet   homes   schools
threat   that's right   Code Orange   good work   scare the shit out of
feed thy enemy   what dumb-ass would do that   **feed thy enemy**   rice
what am I supposed to do with the surplus missiles   chemicals   can't sell to
Saddam again   not in the name of   that mustached Iraqi   cancer   con-
sider what we did for him   put up with   armed him with   gas to kill the
Iranians   the Kurds   you want proof   here's Donald   arm around the
shoulders of the evil   this is too much   **Rice   Roman**   piling up the office
threat   **Feed thy enemy**   Jesus Christ   you can't be serious   fighting with
bags of   **Rice?**   see the ordnance $10 billion worth   compliance   or per-
ish   **Rice**   ye toilers of earth   plastic   duct tape   comply   what to say
to children   very funny   go fight in the desert   in the name of   threat
battlefield still toxic?   radiation after a decade?   tell them to wear masks
suits   detection alarms   leaks?   uh-oh   tell them not to worry a thing

they'll be OK   a little exposure won't hurt   just because I say so   trust me
do the right thing   damn **Rice**   bags keep coming   in thousands   burying
chains shaking   not funny any more Tom   get the media   flash orange on
every screen   panic   duct tape   duck under   threat   every bomb
dropped in Baghdad   a boom for economy   what?   **Rice**   my desk
sagging from   **bags of Rice**   rise in millions   cut   cut programs   cut
welfare   cut dividends   cut booty   no way   **RICE**   Christ   get your
ass over here   John   we need another Patriot Act II   find out who's striking
the iron   **RICE**   Jesus   **RICE**   club them   shock them   cut water
RICE   cut power   cut food stamps   **RICE**   cut bus   schools   cut
Medicaid   **RICE**   what are you doing Laura   cut that symposium   **RICE**
make sure no crazy poets   open their mouths   **RICE**   tape Whitman
tape Dickinson   Baraka   who made them laureates?   strip   what to tell
children   **RICE**   thousands die from bombs   lie   dirty politics   **RICE**
a handful get fat from bombs   what a   **RICE**   lie   how to tell children
die   **RICE**   3,000 missiles   billions of dollars blossom   **RICE**   unite
human races   lie   **RICE**   repeat a hundred times   truth   **RICE**   bomb
them   nuke them   **RICE**   "what I need is"   **RICE**   had I known a
grain of   **RICE**   could   **RICE**   I would have bombed the last   **RICE**
off my face   bomb   **RICE**   exhaust them   **RICE**   physically   **RICE**
emotionally   **RICE**   psychologically   **RICE**   exhausted   **RICE**   mercy
RICE   **RISE**   **ARISE**

SILENT WITNESS

Give back our mother,
      even if she's dry and wrinkled,
          even if her face, once so full of life,
              is swollen from last night's fist,
      please just give her back to us.

Give back our children,
      even if the stars have fled from their eyes,
          even if they no longer look up for rainbows across the sky,
      please give them back to us.

Give us back the door that has never seen a lock,
      and the law without gas chamber or barred window.
Give back the street free of bullets.
And give back the house where children sing and laugh,
      even if the garden has lost all its flowers.

Give back our womb,
      even if it's hysterical from scars and overuse.
Give back our feet, deformed
      from stiletto heels.

And give back our hands, locked
      by a ring of sugar pledge soon to be poisoned.
Oh, don't forget to give back our face,
      even if you've marked it red, purple, blue.

Give back our names,
      even if they've been erased,
      please give them back to us.

Give back our body,
      even if it's been cut into breasts, buttocks,
          vagina, womb, thin waist,
              even if you've swallowed it all,

along with its soul,
please give the skin back to us
even if you've painted it over
ten thousand times . . .

Just give it back.

ON THE BLUE TREASURE PLATEAU

gazelles gather in thousands,
grass scarlet with birth.
Geese feast on placentas,
dropping feces to feed the newborns.

Nomads stand in circles,
arms and legs rising like mist.
"Above 20,000 feet,
we don't sing or dance," they say,
their sunburned cheeks caked with dust,
angelic from all angles.
"The only thing to do is breathe."

On the roof of the earth
where the ocean once reigned,
death is not a crime, and joy
is boiled down to a patch of sky,
soil, beast, snow on rocks,
winding paths under pilgrims' knees . . .

And the body's learning
how to live again.

WET NURSE, MOTHER GOOSE

I had a wet nurse
till I was six months old.
Then—to save money—
my grandma switched me
to powdered milk and rice.
It was the spring of 1958:
The famous three-year famine
loomed over the horizon
but no one saw it coming.
We were all drunk with the plan
to enter communist paradise
in one great leap.

        Whoever has milk is my mother—
        a Chinese saying as old as history.

Every woman can make enough milk
for her children, even if she has a flat chest,
says Doctor Sears in his popular book on babies.

My ex-lover never had his mother's milk.
Neither did his older sister.
Formula was the American fashion for infants.

My sister didn't breast-feed her daughter.
Her mother-in-law argued it was cheaper
to buy baby food than to feed a lactating mother
with fish and meat.

My sisters and I grew up on powdered milk and rice.

To prevent cracked nipples, my sister warned, you must rub them with a towel
every night for two hours. I laughed. How could they ever crack, so brown and
tough? But they did, after two days of sucking by a rosebud mouth.

Driven crazy by the pain,
I went on a spending spree:
Two hundred dollars for a breast pump,
another two hundred for a nurse who taught me
how to slam the baby's mouth onto the nipple.

It's worth it, said the nurse.
Hang on and something good will happen.
Mother's milk makes smarter kids.
Just think of the benefits of breastfeeding:
1. Brings out motherly feelings.
2. Contracts your uterus to its normal size.
3. Relaxes you.
4. Reduces breast cancer.
5. Saves medical bills for the baby.
6. Saves money on formula.
7. Baby learns discipline.

Your milk, she added, is white gold. Don't let it waste.

In old China,
peasants often left their infants to nurse
landlords' kids or sold their white gold
to rich old men who sought immortality.

I want a child, I told my mother.
She looked at me with pity.
"How old are you? Thirty-eight?
I had you when I was eighteen,
and that was considered late."

There was an old woman who lived in a shoe.
She had so many children she didn't know what to do.
She gave them some broth without any bread,
and whipped them all soundly and put them to bed.

In the fifties, women who had more than four kids were "hero mothers"—because of Mao's saying: "More people, more power."

My mother is a model schoolteacher, a hero mother. Her advice for raising children:
Don't spare the stick.
Don't give them too much to eat.
Knock on their heads from time to time
to establish your authority.
If you want them to be loyal and give you their money
don't treat them too well.

My sister had a baby girl.
Her mother-in-law sobbed:
"This is the end of our family line."

> Rock-a-bye, Baby, upon the tree top,
> When the wind blows the cradle will rock;
> When the bough breaks the cradle will fall,
> Down tumbles cradle, Baby and all.

This is the hand of a mother.

This is the hand of a mother
that rocks other people's children.

He has this gesture
    when he is nursing,
        he reaches up with his free hand
            to touch and pat the air, his fingers open
                like wings, and I smack my lips
            pretending to snap them up
        and he looks up and laughs
his toothless laugh.

They say every piece of me is a debt.
My being belongs to my mother who claims
to have carried me inside her for ten-and-a-half months.
I owe lifelong gratitude to my grandma
who changed my diapers and washed my clothes,
owe my health and smooth skin to my wet nurse
who went blind in her old age.
And of course, to my father, the breadwinner,
who worked like a mule till his last breath.
Nothing, nothing I do or give
can pay back their sacrifice.

This is a baby's mouth.

    This is a sucking baby's mouth
    that massages the nipple that stimulates nerves
    that send a message to the mother's pituitary gland
    that secretes the magical hormones
    that travel down the highways of her
    body that tell her which turn to make
    that teach her how to smile at the sucking mouth
    of a baby draped across her belly,
    skin to skin, tummy to tummy,
    cheek to breast.

WHERE THE STORY GOES

Out of the blue,
Claire, the midwife, starts telling
a story passed from her Hmong patient
during the last hours of an arduous labor,
her green eyes clouded by mist,
her lips trembling as if possessed
by the tale's ghost.

When I was five, a refugee in Thailand,
I heard a noise, muffled, sticky,
from a ditch ten yards from my family tent.
I tiptoed over.
There was a little girl, naked,
smaller than my two-year-old sister,
hair and buttocks caked with mud.
She had been climbing.
Her nails, having clawed the wall all night,
had peeled, purple beads of blood on her swollen stubs.
We reached for each other, but the ditch
was bottomless. I ran back home screaming.
Father and Mother grabbed my arms.
"Let her be, girl, let her be.
She must have done something bad in her previous life.
Perhaps her family is hungry, like us.
If it's her fate to be there,
we must not disturb, must not.
Go help your sisters get breakfast. Now!"

I walk away, the voice trailing like a stubborn wraith.
Say something, I tell myself.
Let's sprout a thousand hands, open a thousand eyes
to save all the girls and boys abandoned, hurt.
But I walk away, wordless.
I'm not a Buddha, just a mortal being,
struggling to live, feel sane.

She follows me, the little girl, her body the color of earth,
past the bus stop where teenagers huddle smoking,
over their heads plastic bags with bull's eyes hang on bare trees,
her voice cutting through the ditch, through the mouths
of the Hmong witness, the midwife, splitting
my tongue into a thousand torches
to pass on her story

    which is now mine.

WAYS TO AI 愛

"Love? Can love buy you a decent meal with rice and meat? Can it keep you warm in snow? Safe in a storm?" my grandma would answer whenever I asked about her arranged marriage, her long widowed life.

"Don't even think about 'talking love' before you turn twenty-five, before you join the Communist Party and have made something of your life!" my father warned when I left home at fifteen.

"There's no such thing as love without a reason, just as there is no such thing as hate without a reason." We chanted Mao's words as we spat and kicked at the teachers we had once adored, broke windows, burnt books, beat up Red Guards from a different faction who were once our best friends.

My grandma's favorite dinner story is about a widow who cut chunks of flesh from her arms and thighs to make broth for her dying mother-in-law. Such a filial deed moved the gods so much that they let the old woman revive and live another ten years. As the story proceeded, my mother would bang her chopsticks and rice bowl louder and louder on the table, and finally stomp out. "Have you heard a better love story than that?" my grandma would ask, her cheeks sunk deep in a toothless mouth.

"This is for the burnt rice," my mother said as she whipped us with her bamboo stick. "And this is for the bowl you broke, the corner you didn't sweep, the dirty words that slipped out of your mouth." She aimed at our thighs, where the meat was the thickest, the pain unforgettable. "A filial son comes from under a rod. I want you to remember this, with your flesh. You'll be grateful when you grow up, and you'll pass it on to your children, and next, and next. And this is the best love a mother can give you, kiddos."

I've never written a love poem, nor said the word love—*ai*—in Chinese. When pressed by my Chinese boyfriend, I'd say it in English and French only (He found it cute in the beginning, but later used it as an excuse to dump me). The word sounds like bad luck, too much like a sigh—*ai*. It makes me feel like an old man bent with heavy loads. We say *teng ai* (pain love) to our children, *eng ai* (gratitude love) or *ai qing* (love emotion) between husband and wife, *lian ai* (pity love) to a mistress or a child. Love is conditioned, heavily.

I trace the word on paper. First is the hand, then the roof of a house. This makes sense. You want to keep a firm hand on your shelter, your safety, before you can even start talking about love. Is that why my father warned me over and over again not to "talk love" before I've established myself? Then comes the part "friend." I open my biggest dictionary, *Ocean of Words*. Seventeen years away from China, and I'm losing my mother tongue. It's a complicated system, each word made with two, three, even six different components. No, I'm not wrong, the word does end with a friend, a friend holding up the roof of a house with an assuring hand. So what does it have to do with love? I look back into the dictionary again. It says "love among brothers." OK, brotherly love, love of the same sex before it extends to the other. Then it says "love=adultery." I squirm in my chair. That explains why I've been so reluctant to say "I love you" in my mother tongue. The third item: "love=penny-pinch=greed."

My palms get clammy with cold sweat. The definitions of love in my Chinese dictionary don't seem friendly, and I can't discard them as rubbish, for they are all backed up by Confucius' writing, history, famous poets, and politicians. All of them seem to say: love is a wild animal. Control it or it will tear you apart, drag you into the abyss.

"Don't talk love before you turn twenty-five." How my father knows!

And the companion words—gratitude, respect, duty, pain, pity, addiction, treasure, and many many others—that go side by side with the taboo word *ai*. Are they meant to tame this beast deep in our hearts? Does it mean we Chinese can't love for the sake of love? And if we do, we must love with all the pain, all the duties, all the consequences? Is this how my grandmas, my ancestors, women of my race, found their happiness, though they never met their men before their wedding nights, though their husbands might beat them up, sell them to redeem a debt, took in as many concubines as they could afford, whenever they wanted?

Does it mean I'm hopeless?

"Love?" poofed my mother. "Love is puffed rice. It satisfies you for five minutes. That's all. And men. You can't believe a word they say, they're like commercials. So when you choose a husband, no need to look at his face or crotch, just look into his checking account."

"Love is a wild deer in the forest. It won't return no matter how you call it," my twice-divorced sister said on the phone.

When pressed to remarry, she replied, "Men are like parking spots. All the good ones are taken, and the rest are handicapped."

"It's possible to bear fruit before blossom," my grandma insisted. "Children first, then respect, then love."

I suppose, I suppose, I mutter to myself as my index finger goes up and down the dictionary. Security, responsibility, control, all wise and sound. But something is missing. Suddenly my eyes pop wide. At the bottom is the traditional version of the character *ai:* a hand, a roof, a friend, the usual stuff. Then in the middle, between the friend and roof, stands a heart. It was taken out by the government in the fifties to make Chinese words easier to use.

"That's it!" I shout out loud. That's what's been missing, the heart— 心 —*xin.*

Dot by dot, I try out the newly found character, adding the heart. Memories rush to me from all sides: first crush, first fight, first betrayal, the whipping, the cursing, my mother and grandmas barking their stories to my ears, my ancestors, their ways of love, of hatred, cunning and twisted, with its own wisdom and truth. I thought I'd buried them, to make my life easier, more modern, more western, but they've been living with me, all these years, waiting to come out.

愛—the hand comes first, then the roof, then the heart— 心 . Its three dots spurt and drip like blood over a standing leg. For decades, the heart has been erased from books, papers, magazines. But its pulse has never stopped. It's been pulsing in my grandmas' stories, my sister's waiting for the reunion with her long-lost daughter, in the shafts of sunlight, moonrise, fallen leaves, in the whip my mother carefully placed behind the bedroom door.

"*Ai,*" I sigh as I complete the last stroke. The heart looks a bit squashed between the house and people, a bit fragile under the weight of the roof. But it's there, beating with its own rhythm, its own rules of law. Someday, when the heart takes root again, I'll learn how to say the word, in my native tongue, a sound that can also mean a sigh, an obstacle, a sound soaked with pain and joy.

ACHING FOR BEAUTY

A fine day in autumn   sky as clean as the fields   all crops in the house   wine and
incense for the gods   rice dumplings   scissors   bandages   kneel   to the
Goddess of the Tiny Foot   three kowtows   seven years old   time to bind feet
without the binding   you're only half human   a laughingstock   good only to be
someone's maid   stand on the paper   trace your feet with ink   see how big they
are   five inches and a half   like boats in sail   shame of the family   neighbors'
joke   best luck to marry a beggar   but if you bear some pain   and make your
feet into lotus   you'll have everything   husband   home   children   see the tiny
shoes   pointed like a new moon   more fragrant than a lily   hold it in your palm
how delicate   awe-inspiring   this jade hook   anchors us to a livable place   just
ten months   you'll be a beauty   a woman   like us

Now sit on the stool   soak your feet   in this monkey soup   to soften the bones
your grandma's recipe   aren't you lucky   girl   your dad's favorite   paid gold to
ease your pain   lucky you have everything for lotus feet   thin legs   delicate
ankles   small heels   toes like pearls   stop giggling   open your toes   some
alum in between   to prevent fungus   here's the wrapping   ten feet long   two
inches wide   watch carefully   place one end on the instep   carry it over to the
small toes   bind them once around   leave out the big toe   pull the binding
toward the plantar   hard   push the toes into the sole   to make the front
pointed like a dumpling   sit still   or I'll tie you to a chair   now watch   wrap
the bandage around the heel   tight   a good heel must be round and small   not
spilling over like a goose's behind   bring it back to the front   pull   draw the
heel and toes together   the only way to shorten the foot   into a three-inch
model   screaming already   this is only the beginning   such a spoiled brat
without bound feet   you'll never find a husband   a duckweed floating   can't
live forever in this house   a daughter nothing but spilled water   losing money
business   you know all about that   must have done something in the past   to
pay off the debt with such pain   you think this is unbearable   wait till you
enter your new home   your husband and in-laws   who on earth will hear you
weeping   who will speak for you but your feet   that may win some respect and
pity   so bear it   and watch how I bind   your insurance to happiness   bring
the wrapping back to the front   pull   all the way to the heel   pull again
make the toes bend deep into the sole   push the toes toward the heel   until
they touch   wrap the big toe   pull it upward   pointing like a hook   this will

tickle a man's heart like magic   cry baby   while you can   a pair of tiny feet
two buckets of tears   we all grow up singing this   but hold your body still and
smile   this is how you learn manners   beauty comes out of pain   don't you
know that already   mercy   this is mercy   better to ache now than in your old
age   unmarried   poor   and worse   nameless   this is the best love a mother
can give   a girl must bind her feet just as a boy must study   breathe   while I
sew it up   to keep it tight for a week   put your little claws back in your lap
my hand knows who you are   but not this whip

Here it is   small and pretty   much more refined   wait till I'm through with the
other and dress them both with the red shoes   watch more carefully this time
the secret of binding   takes years to learn   start the bandage from the instep
press all the small toes into the sole   pull them toward the heel   as hard as you
can   bones cracking   feet on fire   as if cut off from the body   I know it all
baby   we've all gone through the same thing   to be a woman   is to be beautiful
to be a beauty   one has to bind her feet   to bind the feet   the only path is
pain   we call it *tuo tan huan gu*   cast off old bones to be born again   you're
lucky   messages   kind words   and monkey bones   I had only stepmother's
curse   forty weeks   bones breaking   toes rotting   no resting or sitting   walk
in circles   stepmother waving a stick   to speed up the breaking   broken glass
folded into the wrapping   rotting   pieces of flesh   peeled off with the bandage
where is my mama   calling to heavens   only silence   no mama   only aching
tuo tan huan gu   to become a woman   to die over and over   for beauty

Now slip into the red shoes   no more old feet   only a trace on paper   on the
altar   a line of shoes   each smaller than the other   the last pair   less than
three inches   by the end of the fortieth week   it will be yours   golden lotus
fragrant lotus   how your father knows   of all his daughters   only you were
taught how to read and write   to give the feet a soul   when he returns from his
trip   your lotus will be made   he'll choose you a good family   a gentleman full
of knowledge   ready to pass the government exams   by the time you become a
high-ranking lady   your feet will bring him even more glory

Eat the dumplings and red beans   grip the writing brushes in your hands   men
are judged by their handwriting   we by footbinding   may your feet be sweet
and fragrant   pointed like these brushes   take the ruler and measure the feet
four inches   an inch and a half gone   congratulations   lift your feet   see how
pointed and narrow   like the tip of winter bamboo   look at the next pair

smaller than this   and the next   even tinier   by the tenth moon   you can
wear the 2.9 inch pair   lotus of divinity   your husband will hold it in his palms
in his mouth   his soul flying in all directions   this will be your face   your sig-
nature   guard it with your life   until you have a husband   sons and daughters
around your knees   then you'll have a foothold   then you'll have a say   then
you'll know a mother's love   wipe your tears   stand and take a step   not too
big   not too small   legs still   like Mount Tai   feet light   like dragonflies   I
know it hurts   burning like hell   but bear it in silence   our secret weapon

INSOMNIA IN DOWNTOWN ST. PAUL

It's three o'clock in the morning

The moon and Venus
have just crossed
over the Mississippi

The only sound
is my son's breathing
through his congested nose

I wait for the dawn
and wonder
why the child is now laughing
in his sleep

I CURSE BECAUSE

You say the streets are paved with gold.
You say even the maids have maids.
If we work hard, our dreams will be fulfilled.
So we come—on foot,
by boats, ships, planes.

"Do me a favor, and get a new name," said my boss. "Something American, like us."

In the alleys and backstreets of Chinatown are job agencies, where opium dens and brothels used to be. We gather behind the barred windows and iron gates, waiting to be dispatched as cooks, dishwashers, delivery boys, as receptionists, waitresses, nannies, housekeepers, button sewers. We work under the table for minimum wage.

First bite of pizza—throw up on the boss's shoes.
Dirty streets littered with the homeless.
No public toilets on American streets.
Can't understand a word, despite my English degree from Beijing University.
Armani suit man spits on the sidewalk.
Pork tastes like woodchips, tomatoes like mud.
Lost in the subway maze.
So high the skyscrapers, so low my basement.
Vast shopping malls, my empty wallet.

"Please, please become an American citizen,"
my brother begged me over the phone,
his voice severed by the long-distance wire.
"This is   the only   way   I can   come   to   America."

To keep my job, I changed my name to Penelope, then Penny. For ten years, I was known as Penny Wan.

Through the barred windows of Ellis Island, we gazed at Manhattan's silhouette. Paradise was only a river away. Around us were the names of the deportees—the sick, low wits, anarchists, criminals, potential prostitutes—names carved into the walls with pens, brushes, nails, knives.

This is how you bus a table, as she stacked dirty plates on her arm.
This is how you serve clients, she grinned, her face a mask of meekness and rage.
If they spit in your face, turn the other cheek.
If they forget to leave a tip, smile and say "Welcome back."
Forget about your Ph.D., having taught in Beijing University.
You start from here, zero, she stamped the ground, hard.

We know the stink and hunger of a ship's hold. We know the unforgiveness of the desert. We may be raped, drowned, dehydrated, caught, deported. May never pay off the loans to the snakeheads. May end up dead in a sealed truck, in the sea, become ghosts in deserts and foreign streets. We know. We know it all. From rumors, stories, eyewitnesses, movies. But we're still coming, like marching ants, locusts, tidal waves. The moon guides us, pulling us to the other shore, by the heart.

The boy knelt into the sand, and kissed the soil of America.

Eight moves within eight months: Flushing, Brooklyn, Elmhurst, Harlem, Elmhurst, Rego Park, Flushing, Flushing. Finally a steady income from a law office—$5 an hour cash, and moved into a house on Farrington Street, Flushing. $200 a month, heat and electricity. Across the street, a Korean brothel. Sharing kitchen and bathroom with a Vietnamese, a Malaysian, two Fu Jian ship jumpers. Our Hong Kong landlady believed in energy saving. Two hours of heat a day— more than enough. Taped our windows with plastic, wore sweaters, coats, hats, and gloves to bed. Fought over the toilet and stove, over who ate what in the refrigerator. But we held out. This was our home. Our dream.

Restaurants and gift shops line Chinatown streets like crows.
I constantly got lost in the maze, even though the Twin Towers
stood a few blocks away.

The u.s. consulate rejected my brother's third application. He talked about borrowing thirty thousand dollars from snakeheads and jumping ship.

Did you have a toilet? bath? hot water?
Could you afford a car? a house? three children?
Color tv? vcr? Laptop?
Could you say whatever you wanted in your own country?

Last stop Flushing. Run up the subway steps. Do not look around. Do not glance at the car purring along Farrington Street. Do not panic at his open fly, pale hand up and down under the wheel, ring gleaming in the moonlight. Do not hear the whispered beckoning: Hey pigtailed China doll, won't you come with me?

"You're in America now, you have nothing to fear," said my sponsor at JFK.

He inches his van through fish and vegetable stands, through underwear, bras, slippers, perfumes, through baseball hats, dragon T-shirts, Chanel bags, through throngs of shoppers and gawking tourists. "Too many Chinese, too many fucking Chinese!" he mutters as he enters the heart of Chinatown.

"Don't tell me it's impossible. I'm willing to wait five, ten years. I'm willing to work, restaurants, laundromats. I just want my daughter to have a good education and freedom to choose where she wants to live, like you, Sister."

5:00 A.M. The old man arrives at Confucius Plaza. Feet apart. Knees bent. Hands before the chest. A ball of fire. Sixty years of tai chi. Under the statue. Never missed a day. Since the ship's arrival. No wife. No children to inherit his savings. He's an American, an overseas Chinese, venerable Laundromat Wong on East Broadway.

> We've been deloused, tagged, marked with chalk.
> We've answered questions like "How many legs does a horse have?"
> We've been stripped, poked in the eyes, ears, private parts.
> When the officer called our names aloud,
> we ran down the steps, screaming,
> into the arms of our estranged fathers, husbands, brothers, and sisters.

Go to Ellis Island. Go find your ancestor on the Wall of Honor. Trace it. Trace with a pencil. On paper. Our ancestors. 500,000 names. More to come. Inscribed. Steeled.

I sent home $400, my first month's earnings as a waitress, along with a photo of myself at the airport, grinning from behind a trunk, two fingers heavenward in the shape of a v.

> What do you really want?
> What more do you want?

PHOENIX CLAWS

From the sink, I watched my sister lean over
our father and embrace him from behind,
her arms around his neck like lotus roots.
One by one, he caressed the fingers
on his bushy chest—a bouquet of
spring chives—tender, delicious.
"With hands like these," he said, "you'll always
have silk to wear and nice things to eat."

I put down the dirty dishes and walked
to our mother. She had taken off her shirt,
and was sucking the brain of the last sea bass,
a mound of bones piled up in front of her face.
Beads of sweat gathered on her neck, shoulders,
and her massive back. My hands,
dripping with suds, reached over to pick up
the skeletons, but rested between the laced bra straps,
in the steaming valley of her golden flesh.
"Get off my back," she roared,
"Are you trying to make me sick
with those cold greasy claws?"

Thirty years later, my hands still stink of
fish and garlic, still chapped and knotted
with cuts, bruises, and scars.
But my sons love them, the hands
that rock, feed, and wash them. They chew
each knuckle as if it were a toy, a pacifier,
a proof of their existence, and they know
it's safe to put them in their mouths.

And I no longer need to hide them
in pockets, or in my own fists.

ORAL

On the last day of school, the professor kissed his student's forehead in the staircase and initiated a romance.

Once a TV crew stopped me on the Lower East Side. They wanted to know what I'd do if I were shut in a room for twenty-four hours with a man. I couldn't say a word. "What a boring question!" I said to myself. "Why would anyone want to be shut in a room with a man?" The woman stuck her microphone under my nose. "How about start with a kiss." Then she ran across the street after a Japanese girl with purple-green hair and six-inch platforms.

He accused her of wiping her mouth whenever they kissed.
"Nothing personal," she said. "I'm just allergic to saliva.
It gives me hives if it stays on my skin longer than thirty seconds."

The baby stuffs everything he can grab in his mouth: coins, toys, seeds, and mud. Yumyumyum, he mumbles with delight. He doesn't know what's clean or dirty. Not yet. He's still in love with things.

The couple stood kissing without a break for twenty-nine hours at a Harley-Davidson Cafe. They won a trip to Paris, and an entry in *Guinness.*

In Paris, people greet each other with four kisses.

The right way to kiss is to touch cheeks and smack lips loudly in the air.

During my first years in New York, I hugged and kissed for real. But people turned their faces so fast that my lips often landed on their necks. Once my girlfriend stopped talking to me. When I confronted her, she confessed that her husband thought I might be a slut. A good girl would never kiss a man's neck, especially when they first meet.

Qin wen: kiss kiss, one colloquial, one bookish.

The root of *qin* 亲 is "parents."

43

The first meaning for *wen* 吻 is lips, animals' especially. When split in two, the character becomes "mouth" and "don't."

I often imagined what it'd be like to kiss or be kissed by parents.

She can't tell him that his kissing robs her breath.

"I want to kiss you," said the retired professor to the student who wanted a reference letter. "But you have fishy breath. Can you brush your teeth first?"

The day she resigned as a receptionist, her boss kissed her and sucked her tongue into his mouth.

She caught him rinsing his mouth with peroxide after sex.

A dirty mouth leads to oral diseases, which lead to diabetes, bad hearts, lung infections, preterm labor.

A deconstructed *qin wen* goes like this:
    Parents kiss mouth not.
    Parents, do not kiss mouth.
    Don't kiss parents' mouth.
    Mouth kiss parents? Don't!
    Kiss parents, not mouth.
    "Do not kiss," mouthed the parents.

Eyes closed, she whispers to her lover's lips: Kiss me.

The child peels the word "ecstasy" from the refrigerator and puts it in his mouth.

STAR MAP

On 7th Avenue in Park Slope
on a bench outside a bakery

My ex-lover watched my son
draped over my breasts
that bulge with blue veins
milk spraying across his face
in a cluster of stars

I wouldn't have thrown such tantrums
If my mother had nursed me
he said suddenly

Then he wept, his hand on my lap

EIGHT THOUSAND MILES OF ROADS

— in memory of Allen Ginsberg

I.
For weeks you've come to my dreams, bodiless.
"What the hell do you know about Tibet?"
you shout, finger pointing in the direction of the High Land,
then at my nose, foam lining your mouth—

the way it happened in 1989.
We had come from different places—
you from Paterson to New York,
me from an island in the East China Sea.
Searching, in our separate ways, for a paradise,
you soaked in songs, Buddha, sex;
I dug the river with my peasant comrades,
hands and feet in icy water, snot frozen
on upper lip, yellow slogans
on red banners fluttering above our heads:
"Straighten the twisted course of the old river
and beautify the earth!"
"Enter the communist paradise with one giant leap!"

How we poured our hot
blood into the glorious cause!

In your 12th Street apartment
I translated the Misty School
poets from China,
Buddha danced on your bedroom wall.
You were talking fast, trying to explain
what had happened to Tibet, what was still happening.
"Things are better now," the Misty poets said.
"No more killing, temples restored, roads repaired."
Suddenly you exploded, finger pointing at my nose:
"What the hell do you know, damn it!
What do you know?"

Silence, stunned faces, blank eyes.
"I'm just translating, Allen."
Bob led you away by the hand.
Misty poets fled to the kitchen,
alone in front of the Buddha, feeling
wronged, your voice thundering in my skull:
"What do you know?"
But how could I know unless I went there?
You returned with two books,
White Shroud and *Collected Poems*.
Opened the covers,
wrote amid the lotus blossoms
"Sorry to yell for Buddha."
You took my hand, lifting it to your mouth.

And I made a vow:
I'd go to Tibet
where your finger pointed.

II.
No rain all night long.
Before dawn broke, you strolled in again,
smiling, your face peaceful after three hours' chanting.
You listened to the babbling, my painful effort to bring out
those faces from the High Land, but words fail
when it comes to the unspeakable,
my stories only phantoms of memory.
Once again you took my hand and pressed it to your lips.
You were also planning a trip with friends, you said,
but the doctor worried about your heart.
I gazed into your eyes, where mist gathered
like wild horses, stormy clouds running
from peak to peak along the Himalayan Range,
energy that overflowed its form and had to spend itself,
like your love, how you loved this city and its people,
moon and clouds, eight thousand miles of roads.

III.

Strange to see you everywhere
as I walked down 2nd Avenue
for the season's last reading at St. Mark's Church.
Your face among spring's trembling leaves,
faces of the dying in the light of a crescent moon
across the abandoned walls, Jersey kids
sticking their fat cheeks out the sunroof of the limousine,
old woman shoving her fist into her mouth to stifle a sob.
Face of the rock on top of Everest
that measures 29,028 feet, the river of stars
splashing across the indigo face of the night
on the last day of May, your face
illuminated with a fire that swells from the gut,
your shirt, scarf, buttons, your hands,
arms, waist, thighs, all flying in different directions
in the heat of joy. It's not about air but earth,
about sinking—to the very bottom—where all is made of
the same substance—then something will happen—
a sunflower bursting.

IV.

You've been with us,
coming and going in flesh and blood,
your body besieged by the solemn faces of death,
We've been sleeping in time's hungry grip;
now you wake, having tossed away possessions,
to enter the soundless—the origin of things.
Our remembrance, and yours,
all taken by the ocean, all given.

> *The bird has reached its nest*
> *in the sun—the key hangs*
> *in the light*
> *on the window.*

OPENING THE FACE

She comes in,
thread between her teeth,
the "lady of wholesome fortune,"
two sons, three daughters,
husband in government service,
parents-in-law healthy and content,
surrounded by laughing grandchildren.
Mother paid her gold to open
my face on my wedding day.

"Sit still," she orders, twining
the cotton thread to test its strength.
"It hurts, but nothing like footbinding,
or the hardship of a newlywed."
She pulls it through her teeth,
lines it against my forehead.
Wet, cold, it furrows into the skin,
into the roots of my virgin down.
The uprooted hair hisses
after the twanging thread.

"Don't make a sound, girl," she whispers
to my drenched face, "not until you bear him a son,
not until you have grandchildren."
She holds her breath as she scrapes
between the eyebrows and lashes, opens
her mouth again when she reaches for the cheek.
"What's ten, twenty, or even thirty years?
We came to this world with nothing but
patience. You have high cheekbones
and a big nose, signs of a man-killer,
but compensated by a round chin.
Just keep your mouth shut, eyes open.
There, there," she leans closer, wiping
beads of tears from my eyelashes.

49

I turn to the light, my face
a burning field.

"Now you're ready for the big day."
Her fingers trace along my cheekbones.
"Your face clean and open.
I'll cover it with a red scarf.
The only person who can lift
the veil is your groom. All other eyes
are evil eyes. Remember, remember."

She puts on her shoes.
"Ah, one more thing," she leans to my ear,
her breath steaming with pickled mustard greens,
yellow rice wine, its bitter sweetness
from years of fermentation in a sealed jar
deep underground. Her secret
tickles the inside of my ear.
"When he sleeps, put your shoes
in his boots and let them sit overnight.
It'll keep him under your thumb, forever."

FRACTURED ALLEGORY, HAND-COPIED MANUAL

Pointed like fingers
arched like eyebrows
soft like the skin of a baby
round like breasts
small like a mouth
red like lips
and mysterious like a virgin's private parts—
this is how a lotus foot maps the beauty of an entire body.

Analogy—
 a lady washing her feet is as magical as flowers blooming in winter.

Ashamed to go out—
 after your husband has just laughed at your extraordinarily big feet.

Can't bear to hear—
 cries of a young girl whose feet are being bound.

False accusation—
 to revile an ugly woman with tiny feet.

Good moments to wash lotus feet—
 under a lamp, slightly drunk, after a dream, when flowers bloom.

Inner thoughts—
 who left the tiny footprints in the snow?

 Twin red shoes, no more than three inches,
 Peonies and butterflies for embroidery.
 Wait till I tell my folks at home:
 I'll mortgage the house, give up the land,
 And wed with tiny feet as planned.

Inappropriate—
 large feet in red shoes.

Love—
>mothers who bind their daughters' feet.

Love medicines—
>extend the tips of your feet beyond the skirt,
>let your lover hold your foot in his palm,
>and place his wine cup in your shoe;
>kick his foot at a drinking party with pretend pique
>until he drops his chopsticks and bends under the table
>to squeeze your jade hooks.

Puzzling—
>a big-footed lady paints white flowers on her shoes.

Unbearable—
>odor of bound feet.

>*A beauty in a boudoir*
>*binds her lotus feet.*
>*A handsome lad walks by,*
>*"Oh my, how tiny your feet are!*
>*Like tender bamboo shoots of winter,*
>*Festival dumplings of May,*
>*but more fragrant and sweeter in every way;*
>*or like the fruit of June, Buddha's hand,*
>*only more elegant, better defined."*
>*"You cheap lustful man!"*
>*The beauty blushes,*
>*spitting as she replies.*
>*"Tonight we'll sleep head to toe,*
>*My lotus feet next to your mouth.*
>*You can taste the tips of my winter bamboo shoots,*
>*and tell me about their sweet fragrance."*

Easy to get—
>a prostitute's shoes.

Annoying—
>   when you're about to wash your feet, a guest arrives without notice.

Untrustworthy—
>   you give shoes away as a love token, but he displays them to his friends.

Pity—
>   a beauty with natural feet.

Too late—
>   to start binding when you're old enough to wed.

>   *Mother, Mother, it's her I must wed,*
>   *her lotus feet snatched my soul, I don't know what to do.*
>   *To have her I'll sell everything I've held,*
>   *so I can place her in my palm, and drink from her shoe.*

Can't stop—
>   once the binding starts.

Distressing—
>   to see someone with small feet thresh rice or serve a woman with big feet.

Speechless—
>   the monk discovers someone has stolen his collection of tiny shoes.

A lazy woman's bindings—
>   stinky like a long, bad essay.

STONES AND BRONZES

In a curtained bamboo bed I awoke,
My thoughts endless, full of sorrow.
No sandalwood incense
To keep my jade urn warm,
No flowing water to accompany a quivering heart.
"Three Tunes of Plum Blossom,"
The sound of flute,
How many spring feelings it has shattered.

Here I am, in a small village near the East China Sea, in a bamboo hut I rented yesterday from a peasant. How did I end up here? Where is my homeland? Where is my house filled with books, paintings, antiques? And where have you been, Mingcheng, my husband?

Can you still recognize me? This crone in a patched robe, how could she be Li Qingzhao, your companion of twenty-five years, scholar and collector, and the finest poet of the Song Dynasty?

Do you know how I have lived all these years, fleeing, always fleeing, from the North to the South, thousands of *li*, chasing our emperor, chased by the Jin Tartars on horses, their fire and swords? Do you know how many corpses I see on the road every day, old and young, emancipated from hunger and cold? Do you know that we've no place to run after this? We've reached the end of the road, the remotest corner of the earth. From here, our emperor will go out to sea in his fleet. But what about us, his hapless subjects? What about me, a widow in poverty, sick and old?

Who planted this banana tree? Its shadow fills the yard. Each leaf folds and unfolds to bare an overflowing heart. And this rain, dripping days on end, makes me weep into my pillow, into the deep night.

Wind and drizzle—their sounds of xiao xiao
Brought out a thousand lines of tears.
The flute player is gone, the jade tower empty,
Heart broken, who can I lean on?
I pluck a plum branch,
But he in the sky, I on earth,
And no one to send it to.

Oh, this hair, so long, so tangled, how can I brush it through? Why am I still sick like this? Sick in my heart, sick for my home, my beloved North, its yellow soil and river, its yellow plateau awash with green forests and white snow. And why can't I forget about you, my husband, for a day, an hour, even for a second?

(Take out the flower from her hair, crumble it.)

The plum blossom has withered, its perfume gone, along with my sandal-wood incense. The only thing still lingering is the fragrance of wine.

(Pour a cup, drink.)

My faithful friend, you help me to forget, to pass the long nights.

(Pour another, toast it to the air.)

For you, my husband. Drink it. It's my birthday. Remember? No? Of course not. You never remembered, except the year we were married. I've stopped being mad long ago. As a man, you were not supposed to bother with such trifles, right? How could I be mad at you? You barely remembered your own birthday, your heart immersed in books, stones, and bronzes.

(Another drink.)

But today is different. Today is my big day. Today I turn fifty.

(Chant solemnly.)

At fifty, one must know the mandate of heaven.

Ha, why that cunning smirk on your face, my dearest? Because Confucius has meant it only for men like you, not for the weaker sex, rouged, dressed in skirts? You don't really give a damn about that, do you? You never did, not for a single moment during our marriage. For twenty-five years we competed as foes and friends: games of poetry, music, painting, memory games, drinking, gambling. I beat you most of the time. You sulked, fumed, asked your friends secretly for help, and never admitted defeat openly, not to my face. But how you boasted to your friends: I married a woman who is the best poet of the Northern Song, the best drinker and gambler!

Remember the year we married, 1101? I was eighteen, you twenty-one. Our dynasty had never seemed so rich, so powerful. The streets of Bianjing were filled with music, dance, art, poetry, and people gathered in restaurants and teahouses, drinking, eating, and playing like there was no tomorrow. Nobody, including our new emperor, a connoisseur of culture, wanted to see the imminent danger from our neighbors along the border. But I did. I saw that our empire could be toppled overnight, crushed under the Jins' horses. In my poem to Zhang Lei, a great poet and politician of our time, I called out how the political wars between the parties were wrecking our country, how the Tartars eyed the riches of our land like a tiger, and how our emperor's offerings of silk and land as peace gestures only increased their appetite. My poems spread throughout the country. People marveled at my poetic talent, but they didn't want to hear the truth. Many frowned upon my boldness to challenge the authority of a venerable poet. Bad manners for a girl from a good family. How relieved I was, on our wedding night, when you held me in your arms and told me you found a companion with the face of a beauty, and the mind of a man!

At fifty, one must know the mandate of heaven.

But our young hearts, carefree like newborn deer, turned away from the looming shadow in the distance, and took delight in the green meadow, the golden sunlight. Our marriage was a union between earth and sky: you, Zhao Mingcheng, son of the grand councilor, student of the Royal Academy with a bright future, and I, daughter of the rites minister, known throughout the capital for my talent. During the day, I read, painted, played music, and wrote poetry, waiting for your twice-a-month holiday from the academy. We drank, filed your collection of antiques, competed at writing poetry, made love. You had a passion for the words inscribed on ancient stones, bronze. It started when you were a boy, and, by twenty, you already had a name as a collector. Your ambition was to make copies of all the ancient inscriptions and compile them into one book. "This book will be the only hope to preserve these treasures before they wear away," you said, stroking the back of my hand on the desk. "And it'll be an arduous project, life-long." "Count me in, darling," I replied quickly. You grabbed my hand, eyes feverish. And I knew, at that moment, our lives were tied, alive or dead.

I've been running since the Jins captured the emperor a decade ago in Bianjing, our old capital. I have abandoned books, paintings, jewelry, fine clothes, and food, even the sacrificial vessels you ordered me to protect with my life. But I kept this, the manuscript you, no, we, compiled together during our marriage, a monumental study of epigraphy, *Jin Shi Lu, Records on Stones and Bronzes,* thirty volumes, thirty years of love and obsession.

Yes, the obsession derived from your passion, our passion. On your day off from the academy, you'd pawn your robes to buy rubbings on the antique market. Your meager allowance could hardly buy anything decent, so I chipped in with my allowance, clothes, jewelry. You brought the treasure home, together with my favorites—pomegranates, pears, peaches, plums. We munched on the fruit over the inscriptions and paintings, mulling over every word and image, arguing over their beauty and flaws, their origin. And it often ended in a betting game. I'd point to a book scattered on the table, bed, floor, piled on the shelves, along the wall, and say: go to page so-and-so and find the quote. The winner got to drink the first cup of tea. And I won, always, because I have an exceptional memory. I remember every book I read, every sound I hear, and every object I touch. I laughed so hard when I saw your face, defeated and defiant at the same time, that I spilled the tea—my grand prize—all over the place.

We both loved wine. Since we couldn't afford it at home, we drank as much as possible whenever we could, at family gatherings, festival feasts, picnic outings with friends, poetry parties. I drank like a man, no, better than men. I've not yet met anyone who can beat me at drinking. When I got tipsy, I'd challenge you and your friends to gambling games, different forms, for I know them all, even invented a few myself, like the famous "Whipping the Horse" game. Oh, how I loved drinking and gambling. The two are inseparable. When I play, I forgo sleep and food, not just for winning, but for the whirlwind that sucks me in. My mind becomes clear, fast, and I forget all the troubles in the world.

> *Remember the dusk at Xiting,*
> *too drunk to find the path home?*
> *We played to our hearts' content,*
> *and steered the boat into the deep of a lotus pond.*
> *Which way to go? Which way to go?*
> *Up to the sky flew startled loons.*

Alas, that was our young life together, full of laughter and luxury. Not the material kind, for we didn't have a mansion filled with gold, jade, furniture, or maids, nor did we have fine clothes, jewelry, delicacies from land or sea. But we had each other, and our joined hearts went to the ancient arts, calligraphy, words from steles, bronze, monuments, pots, bells, washing boards.

Nothing could make us unhappy, not even when your father banished my father from the capital, not even when the same political feud forced your father to resign, and he died five days later, his mansion confiscated, you and your two brothers sent to prison, then to exile. No, we were blindly happy, tucked away in your native town of Qingzhou for ten years—our delayed, prolonged honeymoon. Like a pair of mandarin ducks, we immersed ourselves in our common passion—the labor of research and conservation of antique treasures. Our marriage became the envy of men and women for the years to come—idyllic, fruitful.

Fruitful? Yes! Over those ten years, we gathered the finest private collection in China. Great paintings, calligraphies, and books from all dynasties filled the old mansion, spilling from trunks, shelves. But the seeds of bitterness were sowed when my stomach stayed flat after several years of marriage. At first, you tried to comfort me: we are still young, still have many years to come, and we need to

57

concentrate on the book. Once you turned thirty, however, you talked more and more about your duty as a son to pass on the family name, my duty as a wife to make sure this would happen, and the pressure from your mother for you to choose a concubine. I didn't say a word. At heart, I knew that you knew it takes a man and a woman to conceive; the blame shouldn't fall on me alone. You knew that your real child was the book we'd been compiling, and you needed me, the whole of me—my talent, and knowledge, and my time—to complete the project before it was too late, for the Jin Tartars were ready. They'd been eating into our land and getting closer. Any day, our capital would fall, and we'd have to flee. We didn't have much time left. Not much.

Still, your attitude changed. First you began to frown when I called you "darling." Too intimate, you complained, too inappropriate and a little bit disrespectful. "Darling," I said, "if I don't call you that, who else will? We're husband and wife, for heaven's sake!" That shut you up, but the crack widened. You traveled farther and farther, to the remotest spots and out-of-the-way places in search of the most ancient writings and unusual characters, works hidden in walls and recovered from tombs. You forgot your pining wife at home. How I missed you during those long absences. I drank to pass the cold nights; I wrote love poems to lure you back home.

From a flower stand,
I bought a sprig of budding plums.
Still speckled with beads of teardrops,
Here and there like dusk clouds, morning dew.

Afraid my love may ask who's more fair:
The flower or the face,
I wear it in my hair, aslant,
And tell him to look and compare.

A little humiliating, isn't it, to write so coquettishly at the age of thirty? But I missed you, my darling, missed our bliss in perfect peace, with no desire for glory or gain, missed our simple days when we pawned our clothes to buy calligraphy, how we faced each other weeping for days when we couldn't afford the peony painting we wanted so badly. I'd have been glad to grow old in such a world, but your passion had become an obsession, and your obsession turned you into a different person. Remember that first deep frown on your face when I dropped something on the paper, the first shout from your mouth when I didn't wipe my hands to turn a page? How you forced me to make a clean copy of the document I had soiled? Remember when you started putting padlocks on the library, saying it was for convenience, for preventing thieves? And I, your companion who built this collection with you, had to ask for the keys every time I needed to check a reference, read a book, or look at a painting.

That was no longer an attempt to gain order, darling. It's called possession. Gone were the days of ease and casualness, husband and wife as equal scholars and connoisseurs, a union of work and play. I couldn't bear it. Couldn't. I began to do away with more than one meat in our meals, all finery in my dress; for my hair there were no ornaments of bright pearls or kingfisher feathers, the household had no implements for gilding or embroidery—all this in order to buy a second set of books for myself, so that they could be piled on tables and desks, scattered on pillows and bedding. They may have become stained and dog-eared, but they were being read, cherished, not just locked away in the library, collecting time, dust.

You don't remember, do you? In your feverish pursuit, you no longer saw things, and worse, no longer saw me. When you got a post as a governor in Lai Zhou, you went alone, leaving me behind to look after the books and paintings. Soon the rumors came. You had a concubine and you spent most of your days traveling to places digging antiques. I wasn't shocked. I knew this would happen, sooner or later, for most men would do the same. It was the fashion of the time: to be a man is to have as many women as possible. But I was ashamed: you ignored your duties as a governor, in a time when our country was in great danger, when the people in your prefecture depended on you, like children depending on their parents.

Perhaps you were ashamed, too, of your betrayal? Your infertility? For the girl never conceived, and I heard you sent her back home, right before I joined you. We'd been apart for over a year, the longest in our lives together. But I hardly saw you during my visit. I sat alone in a cold room in that strange city, with rotting windows, broken desk, empty shelves, killing time writing poems behind the closed door, imagining that I made great friends with people who truly appreciated me. How you'd drifted away! How we'd drifted apart!

Three years later, the Jins took the capital and captured our emperor, a connoisseur like you, who'd rather indulge himself in arts and antiques than fight for his country, his people. The Tartars stripped him naked, put a skirt on him, then made him walk on burning coals. When he jumped up and down from the pain, the bells on his ankles jingled and he looked as if he were dancing like a slave girl. Oh the humiliation of his Majesty, our heavenly son! Oh the pain of his scattered subjects who lost everything: homes, families, and people dying on the road, in thousands!

You rushed back home, trying to pack every book, every painting, every vessel. In front of the mountainous volumes, you wept, knowing these things you'd loved so dearly and painfully would soon be yours no longer. Finally, you picked out fifteen cartloads of the most valuable, and ferried them across the Huai River in a string of boats, then the Yangtze, hoping they'd reach Lin An safely, a city in the South we called "paradise on earth," which would become the capital for our new empire, the Southern Song. You kept mumbling we must go back soon to fetch what was left behind. But the news came very quickly: our hometown had been sacked, and our ten rooms of rare books and paintings all reduced to ashes.

At fifty, one must know his destiny.

We moved from place to place for the next two years, always on the run, always packing and unpacking, counting and recounting, until one day, the new emperor's decree summoned you to take charge of Hu Zhou immediately. You sat on the bank, gazing at the boats along the shore, boats that carried your treasure, your life. How handsome you looked that morning in your summer robe, your headband set high on your forehead, your spirit gleaming through your eyes like a tiger! And how I wished you'd turn your gaze at me, even just a glance! But you took off, without even a wave.

"If this town is in danger, what should I do?" I shouted from the shore, my voice croaking with anger, fear.

"Follow the crowd," you answered from afar, hands on hips. "Abandon the household goods first, if you have to, then the old bronzes—but carry the sacrificial vessels for the ancestral temple yourself; live or die with them; don't give them up, ever."

I stood alone, buried in the yellow dust your horse kicked up. Not only was I chained to this fleet of stones and bronzes, but I must also sink with them. Since when had I become part of your collection? And what place did I rank in your eyes? Anger throbbed at my temples. Fear wrenched my stomach: something terrible was going to happen, something terrible.

I waited. The bad news came, faster than I thought. You were ill, but you didn't say how bad it was. I set off immediately, on the fastest boat I could board, and reached you in one day and night. Your fever made you delirious. The following day at dusk, you woke up from the fever, took your brush, and wrote a poem. When you finished, you passed away, with no word at all for the future, for me.

Xun xun mi mi
Leng leng qing qing
Qi qi can can qi qi
Search search seek seek
Cold cold clean clean
Sad sad keen keen sorrow sorrow
A warm spell, then a sudden chill—
Hard to adjust to this season of change.
Two or three cups of weak wine
How they can fight off the evening wind!
The geese are passing—
My heart is breaking—
I've known them from the past.

Mingcheng, Zhao Mingcheng, you knew that even without a war, it's almost impossible for a woman to survive alone. You walked away, taking my heart and soul, but not a single word to your relatives or friends to provide shelter for me. How did you expect me to go on in this crumbling world, an aging, childless widow? What means did I have to carry out your order to preserve this cargo of treasure, a dangerous burden in wartime, a heartbreaking memory? Your last words: "Take care of my antiques"; your last wish: "Die with my vessels." Where was I in your last moment? Where could I go in a time that had no emperor, no land, no hope?

The chrysanthemums are piled on the ground.
Broken, withered, who's going to pick them up?
Clinging to the window,
How am I going to pass this dark night, alone?
Wutong trees soak in the drizzle,
Dripping, dripping into dusk.
Such things, such a moment,
How can a single word—"grief" say it all?

For years, sickness stuck to me: fever, delirium, depression, emaciation of the body, of the soul; lost, angry, terrified. How can I go on? How to go on by myself? Mind spinning, bleeding, wrenching. What am I supposed to do? I call out to you, to heaven. But no answer. Nothing but this abyss, silent, bottomless.

Then he came out of the blue, handsome, young, masculine. Appeared before my death bed in his army attire, his smile assuring: marry me and you'll be safe, forever. I grabbed the offer in my feverish drowning, grabbed it blindly in my utter despair, utter aloneness.

At fifty, one begins to know the heavenly mandate.

My good old Confucius, your teaching is often full of crap, especially when it comes to women. But this time you got it right. Had I been fifty at the time, I might have been wise enough to see through that crook, who married me for the antiques. While I was still delirious, he went through my things, and sold many of them cheap. Thinking I had hidden the most valuable somewhere, he beat me and wouldn't give me food until I handed everything over to him. I bore it with clenched teeth: where else could I go? Then I discovered he stole, not just from me, but also from the soldiers he was in charge of, stole their meager salaries, their food and clothes.

The decision was quickly made: I must bring the crook to court, my only chance to reveal his crime, to get a divorce. I trembled at the thought of the consequences. By Song law, if a wife presses charges against her husband, she automatically gets two years in jail. But the mere thought of staying married to him made me sick. I'd rather bash my head against a stone wall than have his hand on me again.

I walked out of the jail with my hair completely gray. I lost everything: your antiques, my name. Your relatives would have nothing to do with me (not that they ever did before). My friends shied away, afraid that my scandal would stain their good names. And my enemies, those who had been jealous of my poetry and hated my sharp criticism, now laughed in my face. But let me tell you this, Mingcheng: Never have I felt closer to you in my life. Never. You may laugh: How could that be, after my second marriage, a marriage so low, so base. But it was true. I walked out of the jail free: free of the stupid notion that I needed a man to survive, to fill the void of fear, free even from you, my clinging to you as woman, a lesser, inferior species. I walked out of that dungeon a totally different person. I had fallen from being a minister's daughter, a governor's wife, into a wandering refugee, a poor widow who made a meager living as a scribner, a tutor. Yet I blossomed, a flower on the mountain peak, humble and alone, but still a flower on its own stem, whole, proud.

At fifty, one begins to know her destiny.

I've forgiven your folly, our folly. It's too easy to let our passion turn into a disease, our possession turn us into slaves. Your father once warned you: indulging a hobby saps one's will. You nodded, but complained later that it's

62

ridiculous the old man would compare you to those who go after dancing girls, dogs and horses. But a disease is a disease. It makes one ill no matter what it is, just as disasters fall on the noble and poor without discrimination. What does it matter that one hoards books and paintings while the other merely hoards pepper and salt? And it makes no difference that the disease of one is a passion for money, and the other a passion for transmission of knowledge. Both are deluded, both are enslaved.

It's all gone now, my dearest husband. Your collection that once filled the vast mansion, every page saturated with our labor, our love, all lost, painfully, bit by bit. Some reduced to ashes, some returned to the court to save our names from being tainted as traitors, some lost on the road, some stolen, some sold for a few morsels of food, a few days of shelter. I would have once wept, like you, for such a loss. But no more. Where there's a gain, there's a loss; where there's a gathering, a scattering. This is the way things are.

No, not everything is lost. In the old basket is the book of our shared labor, in thirty volumes. They wouldn't be worth much if I put them on the market. Yet I've never felt so rich, so free in spirit. Without the bulk of things, I'm breathing again, talking to you again. My imagination is no longer filled with bitterness. This river of memories flows from my heart, drowning me, fulfilling me, holding me up, sailing me to a new place.

I'm grateful. Grateful for our companionship. For all the unspoken competitions in our lives together. Grateful that you always rose to my challenge, no matter how difficult or humiliating. Remember the days you shut yourself up in a room without food or sleep to come up with sixty poems to rhyme with the song I sent you? Then you sent them to your friend, and he picked three lines from mine: "Who says she's not overwhelmed with sorrow?/When the wind lifts the curtain/she's more frail than the chrysanthemums." Remember those poems I wrote after walking hours along the city wall in the snowstorms? And you always responded with your own, even when you knew they wouldn't be as good. Is that why, my dear husband, you didn't leave a word to guide me as to what I should do, where I could go, who I should seek help from after your departure? Because at the bottom of your heart, you saw me as an equal, a worthy comrade? Is that why, perhaps?

Is that why I loved you, and will love you, in life and in death?

At fifty, I know my destiny.

I've blossomed as a poet. My poems have walked out of the inner chambers, charged into the court, onto the battlefields. I mock the new government's cowardice, handing our land and people to the Jin Tartars for two or three days of peace. I shout to wake up the officials from their indulgence in wine and sex, forgetting that our old emperor is pining away in the hands of the Tartars, our children hungry in exile, our fathers and mothers in the North dying every day. I want to shame our generals into some action, to cross the river and retrieve our lost land.

> *Alive, I want to be a hero among the living.*
> *In death, I strive to be a leader of ghosts.*
> *My blood boils whenever I think of Xiang Yu,*
> *Who'd rather die than flee across the river.*

The rain has stopped. The sun is up. It looks pale from behind the cloud. Still, it's a star. Toast to you, my spring sun.

(Take out the brush, grind the inkwell.)

Mingcheng, my comrade, my husband, you have longed to be remembered. You will, my dearest, but not through your stones or bronzes, not through our books.

(Hang a piece of paper on the wall, write *Jin Shi Lu Hou Xu: Epilogue to the Record of Stones and Bronzes.*)

Your name will live in this epilogue I am writing, in my memory of our love, my record of this human cost to our blind passion.

> The sun is lighting.
> The sun is lighting the path.
> The phoenix is rising.
> She's rising from the terrace.
> Her voice, flickers of fireflies,
> filters through the tissue of air.
> Sound of bells from temples,
> from the deep ashes—the sound
> of the phoenix, yellow, silken,
> from the east.

ADAM'S PRAYER

He laughed.
"Why would I want that?"

Then he dropped to his knees,
hand on the floor, the baby
screaming in the crib.

"May I never be born a woman,
next life, or the life after."

DISTILLED SPIRIT

Didn't know what was going on inside. Just tired, very tired. When she crashed her bike into a tree, she went to the campus clinic. The doctor checked her pulse, studied her face. "Congratulations!" she said. "You have *happiness*. Three months."

Musk placed in the belly button can abort a fetus.

In the darkness of the deserted park, he tried on a condom. The small-size rubber hung over his penis like a plastic bag and he instantly lost his erection. He cursed his fate, her laughter.

After sex, she bandaged her belly button with "Musk and Tiger Bone" plasters and swallowed herbs for diarrhea.

High-class courtesans wore musk around their waists.

"Don't worry," he said as he entered. "If anything happens, I can get a marriage paper for you to show the doctor. Easy. And I'll be there with you."

She would hang herself, jump into a well, or be drowned if she got herself in trouble. In Mao's era, she'd be expelled, fired, cast out.

In the Korean War, Chinese used *renhai zhanshu*—human ocean tactics—to fight the well-equipped American troops. When the first wave of soldiers was gunned down, the second and third waves rushed forward. The dead were praised for building a great wall with their flesh and blood.

You xi (have joy) is a euphemism for pregnancy. Chinese used to believe "More children, more fortune."

Mao honored mothers who had more than four children, and exiled those who suggested birth control and family planning.

The government started its "One child, one family" policy in the seventies, but the population still exploded to 1.5 billion.

The couple waited ten years to reach the official age for marriage (twenty-eight for female and thirty for male). After the wedding, they lived in separate dormitories waiting for an apartment quota.

When her stomach began to show again, she stayed with different relatives to dodge the village leaders. Secretly she hoped to be caught, to be sent to the clinic for an abortion and tubal ligation. She had eight daughters. Tired of hiding like a fugitive, tired of giving birth in other people's pigsties.

"Are you sure? It's only two weeks, for God's sake. Aren't women often irregular?"

Musk deer are hunted for the secretion in their belly buttons.

For two weeks, she went to the bathroom every five minutes to check her panties.

"You're out of your mind," he shouted. "We don't even live in the same country."
"I'll manage."
"How much do you make a month?" he laughed. "Eight hundred? How are you going to feed the baby, keep the job, and go to school full-time?"
"I can send him to my sister in Beijing. It's much cheaper there."
"Find a doctor and we'll split the bill." He hung up.

She called China for herbs that can melt a fetus into a bowl of blood. "No!" said Mother. "The minute I go to the doctor, the whole town will know my daughter is a slut."

She bought a Chinese newspaper, made an appointment with the cheapest doctor in Flushing.

"Full amount up front," said the wife-nurse-secretary.

The doctor went ahead with the procedure even though the sonogram couldn't detect anything in her uterus.

She scraped her daughter's back with a rhinoceros' horn. "Too much poison inside," Mother sighed, watching red blotches and purple blisters emerge on the flesh. "I see a baby appearing between your shoulder blades, his penis hanging between his broken legs. Here's another. Shame! All the boys you've destroyed. When are you going to stop?" she said, scraping her daughter's back, now blistered.

Her Catholic colleague gave her a book on the rhythm method. She hid it under the mattress. When her boyfriend found it, he punched her in the nose.

She charged her daughter ten dollars for the healing.

The pill dries up her vagina and gives her Candida.

He had a vasectomy after his third child was born. Ten years later, he tried to reverse it for his new girlfriend. He got some sperm back, but without tails.

"Please let me keep this one," she wept over the phone.

The nurse handed the newlyweds three bags of condoms. "Are thirty enough for your honeymoon?"

After two accidents within three months, she wanted to end the relationship, but couldn't say it. She began to fart and burp loudly whenever he came close, and her vagina gave off such an offensive odor that he finally stopped coming.

When it was over, the doctor said, "Let's talk about pills. Do you have any preference? Do you want the kind that enlarges your tits?"

The girl screamed on the operating table. "Can't take the pain, eh?" The nurse laughed. "Should have thought about it when you were screwing around."

She conceived her second and third child while wearing a diaphragm.

The secretion stinks in its raw form. Diluted with liquid, it becomes precious medicine and perfume.

With a fake marriage certificate, she went to a hospital. Told to strip and lie down. Something went inside and began sucking and pulling. Drenched in sweat, she tried to count, but couldn't go beyond twenty. So she focused on ten. "Now it's going to hurt a little," said the nurse. Felt her insert a metal instrument, felt it stir around. Something broke inside. She wanted to cry, but held herself back. Saw the nurse prepare a syringe. "To make you labor," she said. "The fetus is too big." An hour later, it was over. Sitting up slowly from the cot. "Can I look at her?" she asked. "Are you sure?" She nodded. Had to say good-bye. The nurse brought out a basin. "A boy. What a pity!" Saw the broken head, ribs, limbs. Wanted to vomit, but held it back.

Before the hunter reaches her, the dying deer chews up her belly button and destroys the secretion.

The nausea returns after two decades.

"Doesn't matter if you write with 'she' or 'I.' People are going to read it as a personal story," warned the professor.

So be it.

ODE TO THE MISSISSIPPI

I want so much to sing
of the Old Man who raised us
with sweat and a curse

All I came up with—
rheumatic fingers
liver spots
a murmuring heart
as stubborn as the universe

SEQUOIA

Because you never die or rot,
you topple, Samson of the earth,
awaiting the fire
to come
for your seeds,
tinier than hummingbirds,
to fly out of
your blazing tongue.

THE PILGRIMS

Can't say
how far it is from Chamdo to Lhasa—
whether it's 800 or 990 *li*.
Lost track of the days traveling like this—

three steps, and a long kowtow.

When asked, we smile, our faces
wrinkled like mountain folds,
our eyes sweeping over distant snowcaps,
rivers, paths, zigzagging barley fields.
Never trained to count miles or days,
but our body knows
how to caress rocks, lumps of soil.

Three steps, hands raised before chest, nose, and forehead,
plunge forward, arms and legs straight.
Raise hands slowly to the sky,
face buried in earth.

This is how we fulfill the vow—
our limbs and torsos measuring the brown path
from Chamdo to Lhasa inch by inch.
We set off on November 10, Tibetan calendar October 4,
leaving our mud house, tent, yaks and sheep to the neighbor,
the whole family on the road, the young, the old.

Gazing outward
at the sky, snow-covered mountains, all things heavenly,
we love each being as we do our mothers,
not just friends, but enemies as well,
not just sheep or cows that give us food,
but also wolves, rats, and flies,
not just the sun, moon, grass,
battered mountains, cracked fields,

but wind, clouds, snowstorms, hail,
landslides, and earthquakes.

We set out, fifteen in total,
vows in our breasts, on our shoulders,
where the warrior god lives and the lamp of life burns.

Three steps, and a full prostration.

A year, a month, three days.
The river filled, dried and refilled,
roads packed, deserted, packed again by merchants.
Can't say how many mountains we've climbed,
how many rivers crossed, nights spent sleepless,
gloves frozen to our hands,
sheepskin gowns torn to shreds.
Can't say how many pairs of wooden gloves have splintered
along the rocky path, how many layers
of callus and frostbite on our foreheads.
On the road of faith,
words of daily life are blasphemous.
Only the six syllables—*Om mani padme hum*—
treasure of the lotus lake,
are the sounds of truth.

How tired we are—

three steps, and a long kowtow!

After each river, each peak,
we measured the distance with a rope and made up the prostrations.
No cheating on the ritual.
How tired!

Three hundred thirty-nine days.

In the distance, two sick ones fall behind,
their gray shadows pressed against the soil.

A lone wolf lurks, awaiting its final leap.
But they stand up, always.

We are tired—
      skin wraps loosely around our bones,
      eyes recede into sockets.
We stand, between the sun and earth,
      our hearts throbbing in the fever of faith.
We take on the pain of each being,
      our backs bent with this terrible weight.
Yet we stand—
      not a cry of complaint or hate,
      not a gesture to show off such a glory.
We stand
      in order to go down again to touch earth.

Wind blows against our cheeks,
      whispering horrors into our ears:
            What if there is no tomorrow or afterlife?
But we plunge with resolution.
Our mouths
      kiss the grass, flowers, dirt, footprints.
Our skin
      turns from pale to brown, from brown to purple.
Our eyes
      so fiercely wrinkled, so bright.

On October 15, Tibetan day,
we arrived, fifteen pilgrims from Chamdo,
outside the gate of Jokang Temple.
As our hands glide across the stone slabs,
crowds become silent, making a path in the middle.
At the sound of our chanting,
the red temple gate opens heavily,
monks lead us through the yard, into the hall.
Under the lotus of Buddha,
we stand still,
redeemed of weakness, of terror.

Mountains tower behind, and our singing
bursts from our coarsened throats,
reaching the unspeakable.

We stand, fifteen in a row!
Our chanting conjures up a forest
in beholders' chests.
Tashi delek! Tashi delek—
blessings from the humble souls
who have shed everything
for a new life.

NIGHT SHIFT

In my dream
My son waved a writing brush
and charged at a windmill
on the bank of the Milky Way.

I woke up.
He was sucking hard
to get the flow.

ZHANGMU

*Zhangmu, a little border town leaning against the foot of the Himalayas, is connected
to Nepal by the Friendship Bridge. Kathmandu is only a half hour away by car.*

Like angels falling into the night of earth,
we descended from eighteen thousand feet
to the bottom, the south foot of Everest.
In two hours, we dropped four thousand meters,
the severe North Face, softened only by mist and thunderclouds,
still towering in the back of our minds,
into a world of excess where plants grow
obese, and flowers bloom madness.
Every corner we turned, waterfalls
bombed onto the roof of our Toyota Land Cruiser.
"This is crazy," Officer Zhang shouted between sneezes.
"The dry air in the high altitude makes me wheeze, and now
I have to breathe this watery air like a fish."

We laughed in sympathy, fearing for our lives
as the car bumped along the zigzagging road.
It was past midnight. The soldier had been
behind the wheel since five in the morning,
barely kept awake by cigarettes and candy.
His boss had built many dams in Tibet,
but never had a chance to cross the bridge.
He was determined to use his three-day vacation
to have a look at foreign devils, taste their food.
At the checkpoint of Dingri, a lieutenant we befriended
forced him to give us a ride.
He agreed, for fear that his Land Cruiser
might be detained at the border.
But soon he and his companions were all smiling
as they listened to my adventures in New York, smoking
Marlboros, chewing Swiss chocolate and beef jerky from Texas.
Officer Zhang kept sighing,
"I'll never have a chance to see New York in this life, never!"

"Perhaps in the next life," I consoled.
"Rubbish! I'm an officer, not a superstitious nomad."
 He chewed the jerky, pondering the dry meat in his hand.
"If there is an afterlife, where and what will I be?
 Whatever it is, I don't want to be a pig or cow,
 ground between someone's filthy teeth."

At two o'clock in the morning, we drove into the town,
 baffled by the blasting rock 'n' roll and neon lights from restaurants.
"This is Zhangmu?" shouted Captain Zhang and his driver,
 their suspicious eyes scanning the tin sheds
 attached to old Tibetan houses along the streets,
 shelves of goods—cloth, soap, cigarettes, and cheap wine
 peeking through doors left ajar.
 The soldiers brought their life savings
 to buy watches, whiskey, and perfume.

I gazed along the tree-covered cliffs.
The sacred Everest was nowhere to be seen,
only the city's flickering lights that sucked
on the mountain like leeches.
So this is the foundation of the sublime Himalayan range,
I said to myself, trying to hold back scowls of disillusion.
How could I ever imagine that those snow-capped peaks,
the highest of all, have a bottom that wallows in the ooze
of mud, dirt, and flattened cats decomposing in the street?
Up there, simplicity takes over space.
Only the brown of rocks, the whiteness of glaciers.
Like gods, those giant peaks
cast their body fluids and waste
at their own feet,
to keep the top clean.

With a heavy heart, we entered the Himalayan Lodge,
two stars in our American guidebook.
A Chengdu girl stood up from a couch,
her powdered face open like a flower.
As soon as she saw the soldiers,

her eyes glistened with ice.
"Full, full," she shouted, arms waving as if shooing flies.
"How about some food?" Officer Zhang pleaded,
"We haven't had a morsel for twelve hours."
"Closed. Time for bed." She stamped her high-heeled shoes,
lifted her miniskirt and threw herself back on the couch,
her plump white ass glaring through her fishnet stockings.
The soldiers took a few steps back, their eyes
popped out at the mounds of naked flesh.
"Run," Captain Zhang ordered, and turned to flee.
We all followed, chased by mocking laughter from the couch.
"Whore," Captain Zhang clenched his teeth.
"Tomorrow I'll have her arrested with no mercy."
We wandered from hotel to hotel, were given
the same answers: "Full. Closed."
Finally the driver pulled out his gun.
"Your place is full? So is this."

We woke up the next morning
amid the chirping of birds and waterfalls.
The wet sun poured through the spiderwebbed skylight.
We ran out, the soldiers' hope aroused
by the colorful stands mushrooming under tin sheds.
"Nepal, let's go to Nepal after breakfast,"
Captain Zhang shouted like a schoolboy.
At customs, he found his friend
who could sneak them across the border
without passports or visas.
I hid my green card
and presented them a fake Chinese ID.
Instead of crossing the Friendship Bridge,
I was taken into a small room
to be interrogated as a "traitor," "smuggler,"
my backpack searched, my journals checked page by page.
While the soldier-travelers cruised around Nepal,
I squatted on a moldy bench,
watching Tibetan workers, Nepalese peddlers,
and Chinese merchants go in and out of the customs gate,

and the bored faces of the soldiers, thinking
"Is this the beautiful Zhangmu
    that everyone told me not to miss? Is this all I got
    from two days waiting at Dingri checkpoint?"

    Then he came along the muddy street,
    ooze splashing around his bare feet,
    but his brown face glowed with the sun and ice
    from Mount Everest, and his lean body moved languidly,
    a leopard roaming the snowcaps.
"Kumar!" I shouted, and flew into the arms of this Sherpa climber.
    We had met at the base-camp of Everest.
"You're an angel, sunlight, gift from the sky," I said, breathless.
    He smiled and told me
    that he was waiting to meet a Swiss expedition team
    before taking them up to the peak.

"How lucky you are," I said listlessly.
"I can't wait to get out of this mess.
    Too much here, too much
    of everything. I can't breathe."

    Kumar looked across the street, his brown feet
    deep in the mud, his eyes caressing
    each pedestrian, stand, house, garbage, the way
    they had caressed me on the North Face.
"Look," he said, "beauty is difficult, but it's there."
    In silence we finished our Nepalese tea,
    I stood up and gave him a hard embrace.
"Kumar. Will we meet again on Everest?"
    He nodded, watching me climb into the Jeep.

"Nothing, nothing there!" the returned soldiers shouted,
    showing me the coconuts they brought from Nepal.
"That country is worse than China.
    Their *momo* bread tasted like mud, their lamb tough like a table leg.
    What a scam!
    By the way, could you take a look at the West End watch?

What's written on the back?
Everyone said English is a guarantee of authenticity.
Hope it's true. We paid damn good money—900 *yuan.*"
I stared at the watch, its steel back
scribbled in gibberish letters,
thinking how I should tell them the truth.

Then I saw Kumar running down the street,
a snow leopard oblivious to its own magnificence.

I pointed at the watch.
"It says: 'Beauty everywhere.'"

AFTERTASTE

Turtle Soup

Tease the turtle with a chopstick until it snaps. Pull to extend its neck, lop off the head with a cleaver. Drip blood into a bowl. Open the belly to clean the intestines. If it's a she, put the eggs back before sewing it up. Steam the blood. When it congeals, cut it into cubes. Boil the turtle three minutes, pour out the scum. Fill the pot with clean water. Boil it with lotus seeds on a slow fire three to four hours till the meat is tender. Add the blood, salt, ice-sugar, threads of ginger and scallion, drops of wine. Serve.

It soothes man's fire, makes him virile, said mother when she passed on the recipe.

Bird on One Foot

She expected gongs and trumpets, firecrackers, kowtows, banquets and drunken crowds teasing her feet with rulers and dirty jokes. But the house was dark and quiet when they arrived. A maid helped her out of the sedan and led her into a room lit by two red lanterns, then left without a word. She wants to wash her dusty face, to rest her aching bones on the bed. She's traveled three days and nights, in a sedan, by boat, sometimes on foot when the road was narrow and steep. But she doesn't know when the groom will walk in. She sits on the edge of the bed, face behind a veil, extending one foot at a time to awaken her sleeping legs. One candle flickers out. The roosters are crowing for the third time, and the sky is turning gray. She lifts the veil to see the room she'll spend the rest of her life in. The most expensive furniture is the bed draped in pink satin curtains, its camphor wood frames carved with dragons soaring above clouds and peach blossoms. Outside, a pale moon crawls from the square yard paved with blue bricks to the northern section of the wife's chamber, its elaborate windows pasted with rice paper and red peony cuttings.

She thinks of her mother's face, streaked with tearful joy. "Smile, even if they strip your shoes, tear off the wrappings." She whispered her last advice through the curtain of her sedan. "The more people see your feet, the more respect you'll get as a wife." And her father and brother, who traveled to the city with her to attend the wedding banquet. Do they know there'll be none? She's not going to be a wife but a concubine, the lowest rank until she bears a son or a new concubine comes in.

She takes off a slipper and sees some blurred figures inside. She brings it under the dim light.

A couple is drinking in a peony garden, naked. Green wine, red lanterns. The woman sits on the man's lap, her scarlet sash scattered across the grass, lotus petals curled behind his waist. He grasps them with both hands, tight, and she totters like a jade hill about to fall.

A poem sewn above the scene, words shaped like mosquitoes:

The Immortals of the Magpie Bridge
The spiritual rhinoceros
stiffens his horn,
While the peony opens wide . . .
the green frog hops
in the waves incessantly.

A young maid watches from behind the peony bushes, her hands in her loosened skirt. Under her tiny feet, another poem:

Wet Moon
Fish sleep,
the moon bathed in the long river.
I hide behind a tree,
see the naked skin of a white moon.

So this is what Mother did for a whole lunar month, in secret, shooing her away when she came close. Blushing, she looks into the other slipper.

She finds a man in the studio, riding a woman on a chair, her red lotuses hanging over his shoulders. She is reading the poem he just finished, the ink still wet and shiny. A maid embraces the master from behind and pushes him deeper into the flower heart:

South Village
Last year in this door,
young girl pink like a peach.
Where is she?
Only petals under the tree
scattered in the wind.

"Wait till your groom comes to the bed and together you can look inside." Mother slipped the shoes onto her feet before the sedan carried her away.

Jade Claws Touching the Cave

She hears him approach, singing loudly. She slips on the shoes. He stops at the bed, hand on the veil. He burps. Smell of liquor, crab, undigested pork. "Red cardinal!" he shouts, catching one foot by the ankle with his right hand. Gingerly he places the heel in his left palm, pressing her plantar between the thumb and forefinger—*the tiger's mouth.* "Oh, how tiny, like the tip of bamboo shoots, festival dumpling of May," he sings and tightens his squeeze. She cries out in pain. "And how fragrant!" he mumbles, inserting the lotus tip into his mouth and nostril.

Conch in Wine Sauce

She wiggles her toe. It took mother two weeks to embroider one shoe. What bad luck to have it soiled by snot on the first night! "Wondrous touch!" he shouts. "Better than the imported snuff." He rubs his nose vigorously, and explodes with sneezes.

He pulls off her shoes and unwinds the wrappings. She winces. No one has seen them naked since she turned nine, after she learned every trick from mother to wash, trim, bind, and dress. A maid enters with a basin, places it at the foot of the bed and leaves. Steam rises, faint and yellowish like pine buds spewing pollen.

One Hundred Lotus Blossoms

Shoes of different sizes, packed in the dowry trunk. 2.9 to 4 inches, pink, red, yellow, blue, lavender . . . Shoes for mother-in-law, sisters-in-law, nieces; shoes for husband, father-in-law, brothers-in-law . . . Black faces, white soles. Embroider during the day, stitch over a lonely lamp. "Endure, my child, endure," said Mother when she cried over blistered fingers. She pulled a graying hair from her scalp, and threaded it through a needle to pierce the blisters. Yellow liquid oozed out along the coarse hair. Mother picked up the sole and said quietly, "You're marrying into a big family. These shoes will pave a long way."

Wild Ducks Alighting on Shoulders

He licks the water dry from her feet, places them on his shoulders. He enters, a tiger leaping down the mountain. She screams without making a sound. Mother never mentioned the pain. Never.

Gold Sticks in Jade House

They swim serenely in a clear chicken soup, salted, spiced with pepper, their silver bodies transparent against the sparkling tofu that floats in the middle, crowned with coriander leaves. The host lights the fire. Blue flames lick the bottom of the fondue. They begin to swim faster. One by one they tunnel into the tofu, still cool inside. The soup boils. The host cuts open the white jade house, now embedded with silver fish that have turned golden. "Please," he says, passing the cubes onto the guests' plates.

Moon Raft

The maid enters again carrying a pot of wine, followed by another with a painted wood box, a bowl of chilled fruits on top. He opens the lid. Eight divisions containing eight foods: ducks' webs cured in wine dregs, shreds of cured pork, ice fish flakes, sliced pullet wings in jellied sauce, lotus seeds, peeled water chestnuts.

"Eat," he gestures with the chopsticks, sipping from the cup placed in her shoe. "When the sun rises, go and meet your 'sisters,' starting from the northern section. They're kind, generous, as long as you know your place as Number Seven. By the way, I sent your father and brother home with five hundred silver coins. Hope they won't blow them all down the pipes, and have enough left to redeem the house and some of the land."

Roast Donkey and Goose Feet

I used to be wild, used to tear off the wrappings when no one was around. Mother would tell me stories. A disobedient girl with big feet would be reborn as a donkey or goose. People would ride me till I was too old to walk, then roast me alive, making me drink soy sauce to spice the meat. If I were reborn as a goose, they'd fatten me up and shut me in a cage, and heat the steel floor. I'd jump up and down until my feet swelled as big as bamboo fans, and they'd chop them off and eat them as a delicacy. I listened in silence, knowing her stories would visit me again and again at night.

Every Step a Lotus Blossom

I sit up in bed, wrap my breasts with a silk sash, and take off the slippers. Warm and fragrant from the night. I look in at the couple intertwined in the peony garden. I look back at the groom snoring with his mouth open. I look down at the bloodstained sheet, which will be displayed as a proof of my virtue. Dawn is breaking through the window. I look at its rice paper, bare and yellowed, no "double happiness" to adorn the newlyweds. So my father knew. So he sold me as a concubine. I clap my hands, praying that the news will never reach Mother.

I unwrap the bandages from my feet, trim the dead skin, pierce the corns, cut the nails. Then I rebind them, tightening each round as the wrap circles from toes to ankle, from ankle to toes. The goal is to block the blood and numb the flesh. I open the trunk and take out a pair of shoes, Mother's gift. I put them on, walk a few steps, watching the phoenixes' wings open on the tips of my shoes. His boots stand on the floor, tall and black. I step in. They reach all the way to my mid-calves. I put on his purple robe, his blue hat. I take a stride, then another. The man still snores in bed, his torso smooth and slender just like mine, only his feet are unbound. I stamp my boots and open the door. Walk into the rising sun. The northern and eastern windows slightly ajar. My new sisters are waiting. But I pass, boots clicking.

OUTSKIRTS

I came here to lose, but the wheel won't let me.

Again, I bet on 3. People gasp. What're the odds for winning eight "straight-ups" in a row?

I snort. At roulette, each spin is new. Would you believe 3 isn't my lucky number? No. Today my wife and I have been separated for three months. Three years ago, she enrolled at Queens College and became a stranger. How did it happen?

"Look at me, Meimei," I ask repeatedly. "I'm the same Tiger you loved against everything. Your parents would rather you die than marry a peddler's son. The night I swam to Hong Kong, you clutched my sleeves, said we'd never part again, dead or alive, if we made it. Your words kept me going. I slept on streets, toiled in restaurants and antique stores until I flew to New York with a fake passport. You waited twelve years, alone, fighting off marriage proposals by faking insanity. Remember how we cried at JFK! Remember the joy over our first condo? My store? The birth of Jia?"

You turned away and said, "I no longer speak Chinese."

I can't fucking believe it.

The wheel stops at 3. Thirty-five to one. I won big. Silence. All eyes wish me dead. I wish myself dead, but everything here—names, dealers, and the noodle stand—solicits memories.

"Dump the bitch," people say. "With your looks and money, you can pick anyone in Chinatown."

But she's my lighthouse. The day I saw the fuzzy hair on her nape, I knew my boat could anchor only in her port.

Another spin. Place chips on 33. Yesterday I called to say happy birthday. She sounded nervous. In the background, someone was reading to Jia. Perfect English. White man's voice. I exploded. "Come back home. Now!"

"Tiger, I need a normal life. I want Jia grow up good, not a hoodlum." She hung up and unplugged the phone.

She thinks I'm a gangster. No matter what I say, she yells, "How could you survive in this town otherwise?" She's desperate. "Those damn tourists stare at me like I'm a whore, always ask why I don't wear gowns with split sides," she cries whenever she comes home.

"Give me a year to sell," I finally said.

"Doesn't matter where you live," she screamed. "*You* are Chinatown."

Bitch!

But she's right. I live there, sell stuff robbed from tombs, wear costumes to amuse tourists. I do whatever it takes to make a living. But are they grateful? The other day, I told Jia to speak Chinese, like a human being. He grimaced and said, "Can't you talk like a grown-up?" I spanked him. He's only five, already imitating devils from school.

I guess it pushed her over the edge.

Fine. We live in America. Spanking isn't hip. I speak Chinglish. My clothes smell like garlic. But does she have to date a white demon, have my son call him "Father"?

I retrieved the gun from the drawer. Cool against my temples.

The ball drops. I won. Two to one. Does it mean I still can't die?

She wants to be in the game, before it's too late.

With her China eyes and yellow skin? With her accented English? She's dreaming!

Does she know she is a walking Chinatown, like me?

But it won't stop her. The stubborn dreamer.

Let's play then, you from Brooklyn, me from *Ruyilou*—the House-of-Anything-You-Wish. I'm piling everything I have on the big red 1. It stands tall, quivering, a pickax hacking into the belly of things.

GREAT SUMMONS

A ritual song from 300 B.C., China, to call the souls of the dead to return home

All names are beautiful.

Benilda Domingo, 37, maintenance, 93rd through 103rd floors.
Milagros Millie Hromada, 35, 98th fl.
Nizam Hafiz, 32, 94th fl.
Oscar Francis Nesbitt, 58, 86th fl.
Colleen Deloughery, 41.
Joseph Ianelli, 28, 94th fl.
Patrice Braut, 31.
Gertrude Alagero.
Rocco A. Medaglia, 49, 104th fl.
Joseph Calandrillo, 49, 99th fl.
Catherine MacRae, 23, 93rd fl.

The sound of calling, voices
of wingless birds
hurling through the open eyes
of children, fingers pointing
heavenward, to the screens.
Big birds? Angels?
Where are they going?

All faces are beautiful.

Leonard J. Snyder, 35.
Christopher Dincuff, 31, 98th fl.
Khalid Shahid, 35, 103rd fl.
Ed Beyea, 42, 27th fl.
Darya Lin, 32, 78th fl.
Lindsay C. Herkness, III, 58, 73rd fl.
Ralph Gerhardt, 33, 105th fl.
Ron Fazio, 57, 99th fl.
Jason DaFazio, 29, 104th fl.
Geoff Campbell, 31, 106th fl.
Wesley Mercer, 70, 44th fl.

City of faces along
shop windows, buses,
subways—the Great Wall
for the missing and the "confirmed."
Fingers combing accordion floors,
air pockets, severed limbs, bones, flesh—
we want them all.

All bodies are beautiful.

Joe Riverso, 34, 107th fl.
Taimour Kahn, 29, 92nd fl.
Scott Hazelcorn, 29, 105th fl.
Christopher Sean Caton, 34, 105th fl.
Brian Monaghan, 21, 96th fl.
Saranya Srinuan, 23, 101st through 104th fl.
Raymond J. Metz, 37, 84th fl.
Joseph Visciano, 22, 89th fl.
Tony Savas, 72, building engineer, WTC 1.
Michael DiAgostino, 41, 105th fl.
Michele M. Reed, 26, 100th fl.
Jody Nichilo, 39, 105th fl.

Let the chanting rise from temples, mosques,
and the bells ring through churches' steeples.
Let the fragrance of bread and coffee
waft from darkened houses, street corners,
to summon the spirits, to bring them home
by charred hands.

Charles Burlingame, plane's captain on American Airlines Flight 77, survived by a
*   wife, a daughter, and a grandson.*
David Charlebois, Washington, the first officer, "handsome and happy and very cen-
*   tered," said his neighbor, Travis White.*
Flight attendant Jennifer Lewis, 38, wife of flight attendant Kenneth Lewis.
Kenneth Lewis, 49, husband of flight attendant Jennifer Lewis.
Bernard Brown, 11, student in Washington. He was embarking on an educational trip
*   to the Channel Islands National Marine Sanctuary near Santa Barbara,*
*   California, as part of a program funded by the National Geographic Society.*

Sarah Clark, 65, sixth-grade teacher in Washington.

Asia Cottom, 11, student in Washington.

James Debeuneure, 58, fifth-grade teacher in Washington.

Rodney Dickens, 11, student in Washington.

Eddie Dillard.

Charles Droz.

Barbara Edwards, 58.

James Joe Ferguson, director of the National Geographic Society's geography education outreach program. He was accompanying the students and teachers to the Channel Islands. "Joe was here at the office until late Monday evening preparing for this trip. It was his goal to make this trip perfect in every way," said John Fahey, Jr., the society's president.

Wilson "Bud" Flagg of Millwood, Virginia, was a retired Navy admiral and retired American Airlines pilot.

Darlene Flagg.

Richard Gabriel.

Ian Gray, 55.

Stanley Hall, 68.

Bryan Jack, 48, senior executive at the Defense Department.

Ann Judge, 49, travel office manager for the National Geographic Society.

Chandler Keller, 29.

Yvonne Kennedy.

Dong Lee.

Leslie A. Whittington, 45, professor of public policy at Georgetown University. She was traveling with her husband, Charles Falkenberg, and their two daughters, Zoe, 8, and Dana, 3, to Los Angeles to catch a connection to Australia. She had been named a visiting fellow at Australian National University.

John Yamnicky, 71.

Vicki Yancey.

Shuyin Yang.

All stories are personal.

Must be told,
and retold till they blossom
between our lips, take root
in the belly button, till the currents
of sap, thicker than blood,
roar in our veins, till eyes

can open again to the blazing sun,
and the moon no longer weeps in the dreams
of children, till every name, face,
every shattered hope, calls
from the womb of memory:

> *"Let some goodness*
> *come out of our deaths.*
> *Let the pain of the living*
> *bear some fruit."*

ON A PLAYGROUND IN BROOKLYN, A RETIRED NEUROLOGIST FROM BEIJING IS CURSING A HENAN GIRL

Sit still, you little pumpkin shitface.
Stop fidgeting. And stop
whining about your sore feet.
If your mother hadn't left you outside
a shoe factory, dumping you like bad luck,
you'd be digging mud and collecting cow dung
in some godforsaken place.
You'd be lucky to have some corn gruel
to fill your stomach, some rags
to cover your ass. And God bless
if your father agreed to send you
to school for two years, just enough
to get a job sewing buttons, embroidering
napkins and tablecloths at some Chinese American joint.
You'd be lucky to marry a peasant from another village,
to have a kid within the quota.
If a boy, you'd be pampered.
If a girl, you'd be cursed and beaten.
Or if you were pretty, which you're not,
you'd sell your flesh at hotels, bus stations,
become some rich man's mistress.
If you were intelligent, which I doubt,
you might get into college,
suck up to your professors for a better grade,
always nodding, smiling
even if you didn't understand or agree.

But this is how fate laughs in our faces.
You, a little nothingness, live in a brownstone
in this filthy rich neighborhood, and I,
a venerable doctor and professor,
wait on you 14 hours a day, 6 days a week, for minimum wage.

You pick at your food like a spoiled princess.
Your Gap outfit and Elefanten shoes
cost more than my daily salary—
all because you call some white-skinned
lawyers Papa and Mama, who hardly see you
except on Sundays, who want you
to speak English without an accent and hopefully
pick up a few Chinese words from your nanny.

No way!
Listen carefully, you little hoof.
A whore is always a whore, just
like a dog will never grow ivory from its jaw.
Born in a peasant's sty, you'll always smell
of mud and straw fermented in piss, your eyes
the cutting wind from the Yellow Plateau,
your feet thick, thighs bulging with muscles,
hips wide for labor, sex, birth,
even though at three and a half you still look
like a two year old, still wobble
when you stand or walk, the back of your head
flat like the bottom of a pan from the orphanage crib.
Believe me. I'm a doctor. I know.
Once a peasant, forever a peasant,
just as a Chinese remains a Chinese
wherever she goes, even in her grave.

Why are you crying, you little oily mouth?
You're not supposed to understand a word.
Two years in America should have wiped out your past,
erased every memory. But who am I kidding?
A night alone on the cement steps of a factory,
a year spent in an orphanage. They say
the trauma has stunted your growth hormones.
But who hasn't gone through a few things in this life?
I've survived two prisons, three labor camps,
the Cultural Revolution, and now this plight
at age sixty, to become a maid for an outcast

to support my good-for-nothing son and his family.
And I'm still standing tall, defiant.

So Lili, my silly pumpkin face,
wipe your nose and walk.
Time to practice again.
You're stubborn, and proud. Good!
Don't ever let your parents' frown seal your lips.
Don't let their butter and steak mush your brain.
You're Chinese, a Chinese peasant girl.
Now take your steps.
It's all right to stumble, to fall.
Here's my hand.
Take it.

I'm your countrywoman.
I am your mother.

HEART AND LIVER

This morning I heard my son murmuring "my sweetheart" to his black Hot Wheel. I burst out laughing. I rarely use such endearments around the house, except when I'm upset about something and become sarcastic. How did he get it right? And where? Growing up, I heard my neighbors call their children "heart and liver," a Chinese endearment for "sweetie" and "precious." My parents called us by our full names. Straightforward. No prefix or suffix attached, like most Chinese do, to reveal any blood relationship or sentiment. They believed that a bad name could evoke evil spirits, and had taken great pains to pick ours. My most beautiful sister got "Sea Cloud," our only brother "Tiger," and our youngest sister, who grew up with her grandparents in Shanghai, was "Swallow." For me, their oldest daughter, they gave a name which has the most common sound, and which can be written with different characters: level, even, safe, flat, dull, ordinary, average, calm, apple, evidence, bottle, duckweed. . . . Most Chinese write my name as apple or duckweed unless I correct them and spell out the two parts of the character stroke by stroke: 1) a body, a cadaver; 2) things that tend to merge and combine. The first sprawls over the second like a bomb shelter.

I never gave it a second thought until I came to the United States. I got used to spelling it out for Americans as soon as I said my name, letter by letter, to avoid being mistaken for Pig, Pin, Pink, or Tin, Ting, Thing. I enjoy making them laugh by imitating the sound of playing ping-pong or golf. When too many people asked me what my name meant exactly, I opened a dictionary and found the following items: screen, shield, shelter, barrier, hold breath. . . . Index finger between the pages, it dawned on me that this was how my parents had chosen to love, by calling my full name, family first, individual second. The name of our father and mother stood at the front of the battlefield—an ancient king (王 =*wang*=king) shielding his soldiers with his body. It was their way of showing "heart and liver" in a time of violence and betrayal.

I put my hand on my son's nape. He stopped breathing for a second, then his body relaxed totally. Sprawling on the couch, he rolled up his shirt to allow my fingers to knead into his back from neck to tailbone, vertebra by vertebra. Two years old, he knows how to love, how to be loved, in the absence of words. A gift still unconditioned, still on the wing.

TSUNAMI CHANT

I'm not a singer, but please
let me sing of the peacemakers
on the streets and internet, your candles
in this darkest moment of night,
your bodies on the steps of government buildings,
your voices from the roots of grasses and trees,
from your pit of conscience.

I'm not a prayer, but please,
please give my voice to the children
in Baghdad, Basra, Afghanistan,
and every other bombed-out place on earth,
your crying out in pain and fear;
please give my hands to the mothers
raking through rubble for food, bodies;
my sight to the cities and fields in smoke;
my tears to the men and women who are brought
home in bags; and please give my ears
to those who refuse to hear the explosions,
who tune only to censored news, official words.

I'm not a citizen, but please
count my vote against the belief
that the American way is the only way,
count it against the blasphemy of freedom,
against a gang of thugs who donned crowns
on their own heads, who live for power
and power only, whose only route is
to deceive and loot, whose mouths move
only to crush, whose hands close
only into a grave.

I'm not a worshiper, but please
accept my faith in those
who refuse to believe in painted lies,

refuse to join this chorus of supreme hypocrisy,
refuse to sell out, to let their conscience sleep,
wither, die. Please accept my faith
in those who cross the bridge for peace,
only to be cursed and spat upon, but keep crossing
anyway, every Wednesday, in rain and snow,
and my faith in those who camp out night after night,
your blood thawing the frozen ground,
your tents flowers of hope in this bleak age.

I don't possess a bomb, don't know
how to shoot or thrust a sword.
All I have is a broken voice,
a heart immense with sorrow.
But please, please take them,
let them be part of this tsunami
of chanting, this chant of awakening.

NOTES

OPENING THE FACE
Open the face (*kai lian*) was an old custom of plucking out the bride's facial hair before the wedding.

STONES AND BRONZES
All the poems in italics are by Li Qingzhao, author's translation.

AFTERTASTE
Most of the subtitles come from ancient menus and sex manuals for the foot-bound.

GREAT SUMMONS
The victims' name list is partial.

TSUNAMI CHANT
For years, groups of Minnesotans have been gathering on both sides of the Lake Street Bridge every Wednesday afternoon and walking across the river as a gesture for peace. Lake Street Bridge spans the Mississippi and connects the cities of St. Paul and Minneapolis.

FUNDER ACKNOWLEDGMENTS

Coffee House Press is an independent nonprofit literary publisher. Our books are made possible through the generous support of grants and gifts from many foundations, corporate giving programs, individuals, and through state and federal support. This project received major funding from the National Endowment for the Arts, a federal agency. Coffee House Press also received support from the Minnesota State Arts Board, through an appropriation by the Minnesota State Legislature; and from grants from the Buuck Family Foundation; the Bush Foundation; the Patrick and Aimee Butler Family Foundation; the Grotto Foundation; Lerner Family Foundation; the McKnight Foundation; the law firm of Schwegman, Lundberg, Woessner & Kluth, P.A.; Target, Marshall Field's, and Mervyn's with support from the Target Foundation; James R. Thorpe Foundation; The Walker Foundation; Wells Fargo Foundation Minnesota; West Group; the Woessner Freeman Foundation; and many individual donors.

This activity is made possible in part by a grant from the Minnesota State Arts Board, through an appropriation by the Minnesota State Legislature and a grant from the National Endowment for the Arts. 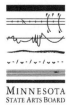 MINNESOTA STATE ARTS BOARD

 NATIONAL ENDOWMENT FOR THE ARTS

To you and our many readers across the country, we send our thanks for your continuing support.

Good books are brewing at coffeehousepress.org